KRYSTALORE CREWS

The Road to Resilience

5 Ways to Have Courageous Confidence in Seasons of Change

First published by Crews Beyond Limits Publishing 2023

Copyright © 2023 by Krystalore Crews

All rights reserved. No part of this publication may be reproduced, stored or transmitted in any form or by any means, electronic, mechanical, photocopying, recording, scanning, or otherwise without written permission from the publisher. It is illegal to copy this book, post it to a website, or distribute it by any other means without permission.

Krystalore Crews asserts the moral right to be identified as the author of this work.

First edition

ISBN: 978-1-7375954-2-7

Typesetting by Marcus Black
Editing by Tami Sanborn
Editing by Jen Bargiel
Editing by Kara Nelson

This book was professionally typeset on Reedsy.
Find out more at reedsy.com

Contents

Foreword		iv
Preface		vii
1	Navigating Life's Marathon	1
2	Resilience Starts at Home	9
3	Breaking Barriers	14
4	Rise and Shine	20
5	Changing Lanes	30
6	Take the Lead	42
7	Heartbreak Hill	49
8	The Turning Point	59
9	Confidence Unleashed	65
10	Consistency in Chaos	73
11	Run With the Pack	80
12	The Finish Line	86
13	The Resilience Revolution	92
About the Author		96

Foreword

Have you ever felt discouraged and wanted to throw in the towel at any point in your life? Maybe you've been hurt, abused, "stabbed" in the back by someone you trusted, or even found yourself questioning purpose in this journey called life. Maybe you've managed to do OK for yourself, but just feel stagnant and stuck as if you're going nowhere fast. If you've ever felt any of the aforementioned sentiments, no need to worry. That's precisely why my dear friend and fellow world changer Krystalore wrote this book for you.

Welcome to "The Road to Resilience: 5 Ways to have Courageous Confidence in Seasons of Change." You hold in your hands a remarkable guide that will empower you to navigate the tumultuous journey of life with unwavering strength and unyielding confidence.

Change is an inevitable part of our existence. It sweeps through our lives like a gust of wind, sometimes gentle and other times fierce. We find ourselves facing unexpected twists and turns, uncertain of what lies ahead. In these moments, resilience becomes our greatest ally, enabling us to adapt, grow, and thrive in the face of adversity.

Throughout this captivating book, you will embark on a transformative journey, uncovering the secrets to building courageous confidence amidst the ever-changing seasons of life. With each turn of the page, you will discover profound insights, practical strategies, and inspiring stories that will ignite a fire within you.

Krystalore, with her incredible wisdom and expertise, will guide you through the five essential pillars of resilience. Drawing from the realms of psychology, spirituality, and personal experiences, she will illuminate your path, providing you with the tools needed to overcome obstacles, conquer fear, and embrace change with open arms.

In this book, you will learn to embrace your inner strength and develop an unshakable belief in your abilities. You will uncover the power of self-compassion, learning to nurture yourself through the challenges that life presents. Krystalore will help you cultivate a growth mindset, transforming setbacks into opportunities for growth and self-discovery. With her guidance, you will develop the ability to adapt, finding new and innovative ways to tackle life's curveballs. Finally, you will discover the importance of building a strong support system, surrounding yourself with uplifting individuals who will walk alongside you during times of change.

"The Road to Resilience" is not just a book; it is a road map, a companion, a beacon of light when the path ahead seems dim. It will empower you to harness your inner resilience, enabling you to rise above any circumstance and become the hero of your own story. You will be inspired to embrace change as an opportunity for growth, to face challenges with unwavering courage, and to emerge from the storms of life stronger and more resilient than ever before.

As you embark on this transformative journey, remember that you are not alone. Within these pages, you will find a community of kindred spirits, all seeking the same goal: to become resilient warriors, ready to conquer the world with courageous confidence. Embrace the teachings, absorb the wisdom, and allow the transformative power of resilience to illuminate your path.

With every chapter you immerse yourself in, remember that you have within you the strength of a thousand suns. You are capable of greatness, and no obstacle is insurmountable. Believe in yourself, trust in the process, and never forget that you are deserving of a life filled with joy, purpose, and unwavering resilience. Now, my dear friend, let us embark on this extraordinary journey together. May "The Road to Resilience" be the guiding light that helps you unlock your true potential and embrace the magnificent possibilities that lie ahead. Now get ready. Prepare your mind and heart for maximum growth, and go learn all of the tools, tactics, and strategies to help you overcome any and every adversity on the road to living your best life. Because YOU CAN!

Marcus Black

Bestselling Author, International Award-Winning Speaker, and Podcast Host

Preface

Welcome to "The Road to Resilience: 5 Ways to Have Courageous Confidence in Seasons of Change." In the following pages, you'll embark on a journey of self-discovery, empowerment, and transformation—a journey that guides you through life's challenges, victories, and unexpected twists.

Life unfolds in seasons, each characterized by its unique blend of opportunities and hurdles. As we navigate these seasons of change, we often find ourselves in the midst of what I refer to as the "messy middle." This is where the unspoken struggles reside—where people rarely reveal their hardships—yet it's also where we confront our vulnerabilities head-on. It's within this messy middle that our most profound growth and strength take root.

I've stood at the crossroads of uncertainty and fear, emerging from these experiences stronger and more resilient. Throughout the pages of this book, I'll share my life's most impactful lessons, interwoven with the Crews Beyond Limits Courageous Confidence Model—a framework designed to unlock your potential and realize your dreams and aspirations. This model will empower you to approach your goals with unshakable boldness, even when faced with adversity.

Your journey to resilience comprises five foundational steps, each building upon the other:

1. Core Values and Identity: Discover your true essence and guiding principles. Unearth the values that illuminate your purpose and

guide your choices.
2. **Confidence and Goal Setting:** Foster unwavering self-belief. Set goals that resonate with your core values, igniting the flame of passion within you.
3. **Consistency with Fitness, Habits, Nutrition, Sleep:** Nurture your well-being through steadfast habits. Prioritize self-care across all facets of your life.
4. **Community and Connection:** Surround yourself with a supportive tribe. Cultivate connections that nurture growth and provide solace during life's challenges.
5. **Celebration of Accomplishments:** Recognize and celebrate your triumphs, regardless of their size. Cultivate gratitude and acknowledge your progress.

Within these pages, you'll encounter stories that may challenge, surprise, and resonate with you. Each narrative holds a lesson—an invitation to embrace vulnerability and extract wisdom from life's challenges. I've never navigated this journey alone, and neither should you. My heartfelt dedication extends to my angels, mentors, and friends who've guided me through life's storms.

In special dedication, I extend my gratitude to my parents Kelli & Bob, whose enduring support shaped my journey. To my family, whose love and encouragement fuel my forward momentum. To my cherished stepdaughter, Ava, a beacon of courage and curiosity. To my beautiful nieces, Emma and Eliana, don't ever dim your light or dull your shine. And to my remarkable Crews Beyond Limits Team—thank you for bringing my wildest ideas to life.

To my husband, Russ Crews, your unwavering love and support have illuminated the path through many of life's challenges. You are my rock and my partner in every sense of the word.

This is more than a book—it's a roadmap to resilience, a compass for navigating the messy middle, and a guide to emerging stronger on the other side. Together, we will shatter the chains of doubt and regret.

Join me on this journey of self-discovery and empowerment. Allow me to be your guide as we embrace the messy middle, harness its lessons, and channel its energy to fuel our growth.

So, let's begin. Let's ignite our inner fire, embody the Crews Beyond Limits Courageous Confidence Model, and embark on a life that truly resonates. Prioritize your well-being—even if it's just for thirty-four minutes each day.

Who wouldn't want a life that's happier, healthier, and profoundly fulfilling? If this resonates with you, keep turning these pages; our journey starts right here.

1

Navigating Life's Marathon

It was a hot and humid spring day in Boston. I had been training for years for this day, but of course I had a nasty cold and was feeling horrible. We're *always* being tested, just as we're about to level up and this day was no different. I had arrived by bus several hours before start time and took in this experience as I rubbed elbows with the other elite athletes. I made it to Boston. It sank in. Walking through the chute to the starting line, I was greeted by extra water stations and a large table full of sunscreen. As the day became hotter, I reached for the sunscreen and covered myself from head to toe. I had my race bag and plenty of snacks. Inside my bag was a red pill. The one I thought would help me feel better because it was an antihistamine. The one that would maybe make me run faster. It was the pill that almost killed me.

All the races leading up to qualify for Boston are typically flat and fast. They build your confidence and prepare you for your fastest run time so you can be good enough that they accept you. Until Boston, where you will run the course of all courses. This is the true test. Heartbreak Hill is around the halfway point and is the highest climb of the race. It separates the men and women from the boys and girls. For those non-runners out there, it's a doozie, to say the least. What goes up must go down, similar to life. Life is like running a series of Heartbreak Hills. You want to go fast and make it to the next level, but as soon as you get "there", there's another hill you must climb. Often, it's even steeper than the last. This time, you are different than you were before. You have more skills, more confidence, and more wisdom.

This is the true test: Will you back down or charge the mountain like a boss? What do you do when things get tough? Your goal may seem like it's at the summit of a steep mountain. It may feel like you will never get to the top. Keep going my friend, and let this book be your tour guide and compass.

I once trained and ran a fifty mile ultramarathon, and most of it was on trails. I learned to scan the next five feet in front of me without stopping or looking down. I learned how to problem solve and predict what was happening in the near future, while still keeping my eye on the prize: the next mile marker. If you freeze, look back, or look down too much you'll trip, fall, and probably break an ankle, taking you out of the race. Where are you looking back in your life? Are you scanning for roots, branches, potholes, or sidewalk cracks? Maybe you keep looking back in the past, behind you? Are you focused on the next mile marker, with your eye on the prize? Are you laser focused, poised, and dialed-in? Are you ready for that next level? Ok, now I know that you are, let's dive in.

At the start of the race in Boston, I was feeling really good! I was at a great pace to qualify for Boston again! If you are a runner, you may know that qualifying and running for the Boston Marathon is like playing in the National Football League or NFL. It's a big deal, and I had trained for years to get to that point. By race day, I still did not feel well. I had done everything I could to be ready and keep my spirits up. I took a lot of vitamin C and drank a ton of water. A friend had suggested I take an antihistamine to make me feel better and it would even help me run faster. I was concerned about breaking the cardinal rule: "never do anything new on race day, ever." This was different. This was The

Boston Marathon and I could barely breathe. I took the medicine despite my inner voice saying not to. I thought, what's the worst that could happen?

Halfway through the race, I was on pace. I was on top of the world. At the top of Heartbreak Hill, I was thinking, "I made it!" I didn't realize this was just the beginning of the day's heartbreak. I started running sideways, my eyesight blurred, and white lights flickered in and out. I started to think I was losing my vision, my heart was pounding, and my legs began to turn to jelly. I began panicking, full on hyperventilating, gasping for every breath.

I was struggling internally, because if you stop, it ruins your run time. I knew it might blow my Boston Marathon qualifier, but just after the half marathon point, I slowed down and stopped at a water station. When I stopped, I was quickly met by a woman named Doris. She told me to lay down. She looked down at me and gave me some water. She asked me some questions as she filled out the back of my race bib with emergency contact information and medications. She was doing her job. After a series of questions, she looked me right in the eye and said, "Legally, I cannot tell you to finish this race. You have to stop. We have to pull you from the race. You can't keep going at this rate. You may not live to see the finish." I gazed up at her with tears filling my eyes. I said, "Doris, do you have any idea what it took for me to get to this moment? For me to get to this point in this race? I was once in a wheelchair and I had to crawl out to be able to even walk one step. I will run and I will finish this race no matter what it takes. I have been working tirelessly since those days to regain my strength. I will crawl if I have to. I will finish this race, and you're going to be in my book someday."

I got up and started walking to see how I would feel. I called my family and I said, "I'm able to breathe and walk, so I'm finishing this race, no matter what." They said, "I love you and I'll see you at the finish line." At that moment, that is what I most needed to hear from them.

Sometimes we just want to feel supported, loved, and surrounded by people that will lift you up and cheer you on. They are your life's angels.

Thirteen grueling, long, hot miles later, I stumbled over the finish line and was greeted by medical personnel, who took off my shoes. They tried to get my heart rate down to a safe level. I was very ill, and I did one thing I vowed to never do — go in a porta potty barefoot. It was devastating, to say the least.

Doris, if you're out there, thank you. Thank you for looking out for me. Thank you for doing your job. I finished that race and received my medal while laying down on a table in the medical tent. That was not quite the way I planned to celebrate at the finish line; however, I was grateful that I listened to my body. I walked to keep my heart rate down so that I could finish safely. It was no longer about having the personal best finishing time, but about taking it one step at a time to a proud healthy finish.

Because I was in such poor shape after Boston, I couldn't celebrate. My wonderful family had traveled with me. They were so proud! We had bought tickets to an after party that we ended up being unable to attend. I spent the rest of the day hugging the toilet seat, while my family enjoyed takeout in the hotel.

Maybe this is you. Have you been told to take a step back, sit out, or worse— stop doing what you love or going after your dream? Maybe you are halfway through your race and have people telling you to stop, to slow down. Maybe they are telling you that you are not well enough, fast enough, fit enough, or strong enough. Maybe they are telling you, "take this pill it'll make you faster, leaner, stronger?" The truth is, there is no magic pill or quick fix to get you there faster. Life is a marathon. It's meant to be endured. Did I have to stop and take a breather? Yes I did. Did I have to walk for a while? Absolutely. Was it worth it? Yes, for me it was.

Twelve years prior to that I had been confined to a wheelchair and had to crawl myself out of a nasty situation. I needed to prove to myself that I had what it takes. When your "why" is big enough, the "how" will show up in your grit, and your resilience. You're stronger than you think.

Life is not a sprint - it is a marathon. It's not a destination, but a journey and you must take one step at a time, one day at a time. If you're feeling ready to quit, don't. In the running world, they call that a DNF, which stands for "did not finish." You're disqualified. You don't get a medal. You don't get to feel a sense of accomplishment. You don't get to see the finish line. You don't get to celebrate.

Maybe it's time for you to get back up. No matter how tired you are, you've got to keep yourself in the race. You must not tap out. Some miles are going to be harder than others. In fact, most miles are harder than you ever imagined. Most elite athletes have more bad days than they have good days. I began to realize that when someone tells me to slow down or stop, it's triggering for me. I use it as a challenge instead. I view it as a chance to show up and prove to myself and others what I am capable of.

After Boston, I just kept going. I ran more marathons, trying to achieve more, and get more medals. I racked up the miles, and escaped. I traveled the world. I was an overachiever. My nervous system was so used to keeping the momentum going until I couldn't go anymore. As overachievers we just do. We don't slow down. We challenge ourselves to be better.

Where in life are you over achieving? Are you reaching for that next thing and finding yourself hugging the toilet seat, perhaps overwhelmed and burned out? You put your head down, you dive in. You reflect and you keep going on to the next one for the next big challenge. You beat yourself up, but keep pushing. I had strung several marathons together when people expressed their concerns saying things like, "that was a tough race" or "maybe you shouldn't run so much" or "you should slow down". For many years, no one asked me why I ran so much. In fact, I didn't really ask myself why I did it, I just kept running like Forrest

Gump. I was surrounded by all the other crazy runners who "got it". Then one New Year's Eve, I looked down at my eight marathon finisher medals to celebrate my accomplishments for that year, and realized I wasn't happy with myself. Then and there, I vowed to figure out why. Why do I run so much? What was I running for? What or who was I running from? There certainly weren't any bears chasing me. Why did I love running so much?

I started to answer some of these questions internally. Part of it was the challenge, I knew I could push myself to the limits. I turned into a mad scientist with my body, and I learned about nutrition and hydration. I also learned about the power of rest and recovery. I found that running was just me, my thoughts, my dreams, and my experiences. I spent a lot of time alone challenging myself, questioning myself, doubting myself, but also cheering myself on. This is the power of running. I started paying attention and asking myself a few powerful questions. What am I escaping from? What is the feeling that I get out of it? What is the impact that it has? Why a marathon?

The marathon is like life. The majority of the work is done before the race even starts, and race day is just a victory lap. It's a test of all the hard work, the accomplishments, the resilience, and it leads to triumph despite training on the days when it was cold, when it was rainy, when there was a blizzard, when it was icy, when it was hot, and when it was humid. Other powerful lessons learned were when my nutrition and hydration wasn't on point because I had a couple glasses of wine or greasy food the night before. In the end, I found that the biggest thing I was running for was freedom.

Picture this: your feet hitting the pavement, creating a rhythm that syncs with your heartbeat. Running isn't just about movement; it's about breaking free, gaining control, and feeling alive. It's like your own personal escape, where you leave behind vulnerability and those not-so-great relationships. With every step, you're saying, "I'm in charge now." The wind in your hair feels like a high-five from the universe, cheering you on as you run toward empowerment. You're not just running; you're rewriting your story, turning the road into your playground of self-discovery. As you conquer each mile, you're not just covering distance—you're embracing freedom with every stride.

Things started to change when people began spending time with me and really asking me powerful questions. I had the answers because I had done the internal reflection work. I couldn't wait to share them. Most marathoners and runners are so excited to share about their trials and tribulations and the times where they almost crapped their pants. Yes, I have those stories too. And yes, I've crapped my pants, but this book is not about that. What I learned was to spend five minutes with someone before judging. If you spend five minutes with me you'll realize I pooped today too. I am a real human with real struggles, real dreams, real goals, and real experiences, just like you.

Once you start to spend time with someone, you get to know their real story. Not the one on the internet, not the highlight reel. It's never what you think, it's always much deeper than that. People want to be seen, feel valued, heard, trusted, and that they belong. What I found was the more I ran, the more disconnected I felt. But it wasn't until some sweet angels (you know who you are) asked me "Why do you run? Why do you do what you do? There has got to be more to the story".

Are you a little "too much" or "extra" for people? I sure am, and people have let me know every single day of my life. I have learned that everyone has an opinion and that opinion has nothing to do with me. Some are willing to listen first before they judge. These are the angels. For the first time, I felt like I could share my story about why I keep going amidst all the struggles, the adversity, and all the people telling me to stop. This isn't their fault - it's all they know.

This book will definitely give you a glimpse into a day of walking a few miles in my shoes. If you're in a season of change right now, it might feel like everything is working against you. You may not know what to do next. Remember that it just takes one step. Let me and this book be your guide. It's a journey and you may be feeling alone, frustrated, and overwhelmed. Put your seatbelt on, because it's a wild ride. This journey of life has its ups and downs, and there are some MAJOR potholes and traffic stops. There is also a way to embrace the chaos and live a fulfilling life. I promise it is possible. Keep reading. Don't DNF this book or your life. Promise?? No really, pinky swear right now. And let's dive in.

The key is to keep going and get back up every single time, no matter what. Keep trying. Keep doing. Know your "why". Like your life depends on it. Because it does.

* * *

Crews Beyond Limits Journal Prompts:

1. Share a story of a time when you demonstrated discipline in pursuit of a challenging goal. How did your commitment shape the journey and the final result?
2. Describe a goal you've been working towards. What obstacles have you encountered along the way, and how can you continue to push forward?
3. Think about a role model who embodies persistence. What qualities do they possess that inspire you to overcome setbacks?

2

Resilience Starts at Home

Growing up, we had a big console television in our living room with only thirteen channels. I have vivid memories of looking up to my role model, my mom, like the superhero that she is. In addition to VHS tapes of every Richard Simmons and Gilad video available, she had every piece of equipment from thigh masters to ankle weights to the Shake Weight. She lived in front of our television, before and after work. She would dance, sweat, and laugh, and it was here where she came alive.

Sometimes I joined her, or at least dressed up to workout with her. I had my own set of hand weights and outfits. I remember backdrops of beautiful beaches, mountains, waterfronts, sunsets, and sunrises. The fitness pros were teaching my mom skills from a platform in the middle of the ocean. It seemed like heaven, and definitely something for the rich and famous. It didn't seem real. I watched her as she moved her body every single day, without fail. At times I would make fun of her, because I didn't get it back then. She would challenge herself, dance like nobody was watching, and sing along - she has a beautiful voice. I was always watching.

I was seven when my parents separated. From a young age, my mom raised me and my younger brother, with the help of my Oma (Grandma). She was a single mother working full time. She earned her Associate's degree and worked tirelessly to provide for us. My mom signed me up for dance as soon as I could walk. I never missed a day of practice or a recital. I loved how I felt in tutus, the lace socks, and jelly shoes. I had every color of those jelly shoes. I would perform for my family, dancing and prancing around. I used my mom's workout equipment and would mimic the moves she made. I wanted to be just like her. She is beautiful, generous, kind, and has a loving heart. In my hometown of Buffalo, New York, she is like the mayor - everyone knows Mama Kelli. She is radiant like a ray of sunshine. She shows up to serve her loved ones, family, friends, and community consistently, no matter what.

My mom is my superhero. I have never really seen the human side of her - she has always only shown her confidence. She has always put a smile on her face and worked out every single day. She has always taken care of her body, her nutrition, and never faltered in her routine. Her consistency creates so much confidence, so much poise, so much positive energy that surrounds her. She has created a legacy and has left a mark on everyone's heart.

My mom's knight in shining armor appeared at the beach one day. Going against her inner chatter, she began talking to this man. He was intriguing, fit, strong, and a little intimidating. He wore jeans and no shirt and motorcycle boots. He rolled up on a Harley with hair flying in the wind like Fabio, but he looked like macho man Randy Savage. This man was the missing puzzle piece for her and our family. Bob is the man I proudly call Dad. He is consistent, incredibly structured, and organized. He loves his routine. He's been working out in his basement since he was sixteen. Bob has continued with this consistency to this day and thankfully my mom has done the same. Both have honored their non-negotiables all while blending families and navigating careers. I remember my dad picking us up from school and sports practice, and being at every concert or game. He was always present, kind, loving and supportive, everything I could want in a dad. He also put a smile on my mom's face, which was a huge bonus. My parents shared a love for the beach, which I have inherited from them as well.

My parents worked tirelessly when they had no money, in an effort to build a life where we didn't have to worry about going without. We collected cans almost every day. We would pick the garbage, go into dumpsters and then turn in our cans. I learned at a young age that hard work turned into money. What I didn't realize was that hard work helped us experience a life that we never could have otherwise imagined. We got to see the world. We got to travel with the money we collected. We would go to Ocean City or Virginia Beach during our summer break from school. We got to see life outside our small island town. Through these experiences, I learned that anything is possible. We also learned about different cultures, languages, and ways of living to open up our perspective of the world.

My parents learned and grew together, and they dreamed big. They took a community class on how to buy stock, bought Kmart stock for $1, and together, they learned to grow their empire. This taught me so much about creating a vision, hard work, being in a partnership, and going all in, without knowing what the future will hold. They stuck to their standards and they always showed up for their health and their fitness first. Together, they experienced challenges and handled the tough conversations which included financial struggles, divorce, family abandonment, death, grief, health challenges, and addiction. Still, they showed up for each other, no matter what.

Our family theme is that we are hardworking, healthy, active, loving, and charismatic. We really are the life of the party and it doesn't start until we show up. Growing up in our household we didn't have many snacks, soda or junk food. When we did, it was a special occasion. I'll never forget the days when my parents would juice fruits and vegetables and make us drink this tall glass of green juice. If we were good, we would get extra apples in it to make it taste sweeter. Even still, I loathed the taste of it. There were times that my brother and I would work together with a master plan to distract our parents so we could sneak to the bathroom and dump the glass down the toilet. We would do anything to avoid drinking the green juice. Maybe I'd be taller if I drank more green juice, but who knows? I can't change the past, but I can control how I use these lessons to fuel my body and be healthier for the future.

As I mentioned, I never really saw my mom very vulnerable as a kid. She forged through the marathon of life's challenges, and was always a positive problem solver. As I grew older, I learned that I had many of the same qualities and that the apple doesn't fall too far from the tree. I love the tree and all the roots and branches. We all must bloom where we are planted. I learned that many high performers, perfectionists, people pleasers, and athletes are expected to be "on" all the time. It's hard to show the struggles, challenges, and pain behind the smile. Everyone expects you to be the life of the party, to be smiling and positive all the time. What if they saw me cry? What if they saw me frustrated or upset? What if I did not have the answers? Would I look weak? Could they handle the truth if I could show my true self? How to respond? Would they pity me? Rather than risking what those answers are, we just keep going. Rub some dirt on it. In the military, they say embrace the suck. In dance, gymnastics, and cheerleading, the show must go on. We put a smile on, get on stage, the lights come on, we continue. But the thing is, we can only suck it up for so long. The party always comes to an end.

During the lonely nights and the silent moments, stressors and pressure build up like a storm. The empty calendar is a breeding ground for the devil to creep in. He loves when you're alone. All of the doubt, shame, guilt, overwhelm, fear, uncertainty, abandonment, challenges, the noise, and other people's opinions hit like a monsoon. Everything you've done, all the things you said but didn't mean, and all the negative thoughts flood your mind when it gets quiet. It's not for the faint at heart.

When this happens, you can choose to be a victim or a victor. In these moments, it's important to identify your non-negotiables and engage in self care more than ever. Determine what is in your tool belt. Think about your fitness, your health, your sleep, your hydration, your movement, and your willingness to do what it takes. You are not your past. You're not a victim. You've made it through 100% of the hard days. It's a slippery slope and shame is only fueled by silence and loneliness. You can't feel guilt unless you have someone else who makes you feel that way.

Practicing self love, grace, gratitude, and forgiveness is so important. When you identify your values and your non-negotiables, anything is possible. You're unstoppable, unshakeable, unbreakable. We only get one body, one mind, one heart, one shot. Life is a journey, and it's going to be a roller coaster of emotions, challenges, disappointments, and triumphs. Sometimes you have to stand up and be your own knight in shining armor. It's hard. It's uncomfortable. It's worth it. You're worth it. Believe this like your life depends on it, because it does.

* * *

Crews Beyond Limits Journal Prompts:

1. Think about a role model who embodies persistence. What qualities do they possess that inspire you to overcome setbacks?
2. Explore the link between healthy habits and personal growth. How do these habits contribute to your resilience, confidence, and pursuit of excellence?
3. Describe your ideal self-care routine. How can you integrate small, consistent practices into your daily life to nurture your physical, mental, and emotional health?

3

Breaking Barriers

I shook my Master Sense's hand as he handed me the graduation certificate. I had earned the next belt in Karate. I had a proud but stern grin on my face as I shook his hand. We were in the basement of a kindergarten school in a church, where an American flag hung on the wall. I smiled with pride as I earned my green belt. My hair was neat, slicked back and professional. At a young age of just eleven years old, I had learned emotional intelligence, discipline, consistency, and teamwork. I also learned to drill self defense moves that I never thought I would use. When we trained we never touched each other, as it was all self defense. We would do floor work on the mats, and, yes, they were stinky. Maybe you have children around the teenage years and probably have a stench ingrained in your soul. And just like wrestlers, you can imagine the skin conditions you get from the mats and not wearing shoes. I was the only female, but I was proud. I developed skills and tools to hang with the boys.

I went to high school without a serious steady boyfriend. I dated here and there but I had this pressure to find a nice boy with a nice family. The goals and rules were to graduate college, don't dorm, live at home. Then get a good job, be a good girl, don't get in trouble, and don't call attention to yourself. After prom, I started dating someone, went to college, and got a good job working in restaurants part time, while working through my undergrad program full time. My first week of college was in early September of 2001. During my first week of college I stood in the student union as I watched the devastating news that had happened on 9/11. My friend and I joined the military after that to serve our country part time while helping to pay for school. When I returned from my training, I went back to college full time. I was an athlete running indoor track and cheerleading, and served part time in the Air National Guard.

At first my boyfriend was supportive and I thought all along that he was a nice guy, with a nice family. He was, until he started seeing my success, my travel for the military, and my being around other men. As his insecurities grew, my confidence shrank more day by day. There was always a competition. Competition of who had more success and who was allowed to do certain things. This man had a nice family and he was a nice guy, so I did what I thought I needed. I was nice to him. I did not stand out. I went to church on Sundays, had family dinners and showed up to the parties looking good. At this point in my life, I was torn in several different directions. We finished our undergrad together and we were looking at our next steps for master's programs.

I thought, hey, I could go to law school and get an MBA, so I researched joint JD/MBA programs. I'll never forget the phone call I made to him while I was at work on lunch break. I was so excited about the program that I had found. He said "you can't go to law school. Law school is too hard for you. That's my dream." I hung up the phone. And my dreams were crushed for law school before even taking the LSAT.

I began noticing the red flags. By then, I had so much loyalty and many years invested in our relationship, and I was comfortable. I thought I was happy at the time. We attended work parties. We had mutual friends. He started going to bars and staying out later. There were arguments in public about what kind of job everyone had and what kind of car everyone drove. It was a constant competition. Everywhere we went all of a sudden it mattered how much money everyone was making and who had the nicer suit. Something didn't feel right. His insecurities continued to grow and his behavior escalated. I began to feel worried for my safety. Once, at his work Christmas party, he had too much to drink. Dark liquor never agreed with him. After a few drinks, his coworkers looked at me with worried looks on their faces. One of them gave me his car keys and said "I don't think it's good for him to drive." I agreed and put them in my purse. We enjoyed the Christmas party conversations with the other spouses. About ten minutes later, he came looking for me asking for his keys. I was scared when I saw the rage in his eyes. He was so angry. I tried to calm him down and tell him that it's not a good idea for him to drive home. He got even more angry. I tried to walk away and walk out the door to get some fresh air, because we were making a scene. He followed me, put me over his shoulder and carried me down the street. There was an ice cream store next door and a large brick building and an alley. He was not taking me for ice cream that night. Instead, I found myself up against that brick building being held by my throat. He screamed at me, "Where are my keys? Where are my keys? You stole them, you stole them." I tried to explain, but I could barely even talk. I could not breathe. All I could do was try to scream. Thank God his coworkers were outside smoking. They heard my screaming and came to my rescue. The next day, he gave me an iPod in a bag and a necklace. In an effort of an apology he would slide his credit card across the desk. "Go shopping for whatever you need or want". This was his pattern. I didn't realize what it was doing to my confidence, my self esteem, and worthiness. I believed I had met a nice man, with a nice family. I never thought that one day I'd have to use some of those self defense techniques I learned at eleven years old on someone who I thought cared about me.

 I made it as an NFL Cheerleader during my senior year of my undergraduate program. I was so proud! I soon realized he was not so proud. I wasn't allowed to hang out with the girls after practice because I had to come straight home. It was an amazing experience nonetheless and the girls never treated me differently. They understood; however, it did cost me deeper relationships with my teammates though. He definitely made the experience a challenge. He was publicly verbal about his disappointment that we were not getting paid for the work that we were doing as cheerleaders and as role models in the community.

I was serving in the military at the time of my NFL season. I would go to promotional events, autograph signings, and community service events. I was selected to go overseas to meet the troops in Afghanistan. It was a special nomination to select a deserving cheerleader, but I had to decline. I wasn't allowed to "subject myself to soldiers" because my uniform showed my midsection. My brothers and sisters in arms who were overseas did not get a visit by me. Someone else went in my place.

I had finally had enough. I began going to therapy when he thought I was going to dinner with friends. I knew I needed help to have the courage to walk away. I wrote him letters to heal and get my thoughts and emotions out. I felt so powerless in attempting to have a conversation about our relationship. I found that writing helped me process and sort out my emotions in a healthy way. Studies show that eighty six percent of people are visual learners. It's no wonder why getting my emotions and facts on paper helped me see the bigger picture. I never gave him the letters or got the closure and last word that I desperately wanted. However, I knew I needed to get out of my head and more importantly, that relationship. I vowed to stay single for a very long time. I needed to date myself. I needed to find myself, love myself again, and figure out who I was deep to the core. I had been called a girlfriend, among many other choice words, for six years. I didn't quite understand what was happening at the time. I just knew that he wasn't the one. There was a big misalignment with priorities and values. I'm proud of myself for following my gut and having the courage to leave.

Have you ever been in a relationship that you feel you can't get out of? Is there a misalignment with values? Is money always an object of discussion and disagreement? How do we choose our partners at such a young age without knowing what their values will be? How can we guarantee that there will be no insecurity and jealousy? When you're so far in a relationship, you can't always see past the clouds. It's easier to stay in it, safe and comfortable. So that's what I did, until I realized that I was made for more. And so are you.

I started taking fitness and kickboxing classes at the gym. I built my strength and confidence, and was feeling healthier and free. I began to regain my independence as I healed from the inside out. I spent an enormous amount of time alone traveling and building my military career, tirelessly trying to prove myself and my worth through my work. I volunteered for projects and travel opportunities. One of these led to training in IT project management in Biloxi, Mississippi for almost a year. I moved everything down there and really had a great time. I was learning so much about computer engineering, binary programming, and electrical circuits. It was most intriguing to me that I knew what happened when I sent an email or when I plugged my hair dryer in. I built a computer and telephone network on a whiteboard, and made it come alive in a remote location. My brain works well visually with a whiteboard and a problem to solve.

I was the only woman and I didn't feel like I fit in. I shocked all the guys in the class. They couldn't believe that a woman was qualified to do what they could. Even though I was cool in their book, I still couldn't hang out with them outside of school because they were considered "pipeline students," fresh out of basic military training. While they were building computer networks in the dorms on their off time, I would go to all the casinos after school as they cater to out of state residents. My players card got me tons of free dinners, hotel rooms, and concerts. At least once a week I stayed at the Hard Rock Casino. They had an awesome swim up bar and pool party on Sundays, and I met some great people.

By then, I was used to doing most things on my own. It gave me a lot of time to reflect and process. I'm grateful for therapy. I'm grateful for the self defense techniques that I learned. What I can do is be alert, listen to my gut intuition, and make sure I have a plan. The only thing I can do is control what I can control, and not live in fear. And when the time comes, I need to pivot. I need to know myself to the core, and be confident. I grew a tougher outer core, I learned to be aware, have a plan, and have tools in my toolkit to keep going no matter what, like my life depends on it. Because it does.

* * *

Crews Beyond Limits Journal Prompts:

1. List three qualities that you believe are essential in a supportive and nurturing relationship. Reflect on how these qualities contribute to a strong foundation of trust and connection.
2. Reflect on a time when you allowed someone else's opinion to influence a significant decision regarding your dreams or goals. How did this choice make you feel in the short term and in the long run? Consider what you gained and lost from this experience, and how it shaped your perspective on following your own path.
3. Explore how setting boundaries can be an act of self-love and a way to honor your own needs. How can you encourage other women to establish their own boundaries as an essential aspect of their journey towards independence and self-care?

4

Rise and Shine

I remember the day my coworker told me about a new organization that was just starting up in the area. He said, "Krystal, you like to run and work out all the time, why don't you check this out? Here's the website www.teamrwb.org." It seemed like a really great initiative, so I looked into it. They did not have a big social media presence and the only event that was published was a bowling event. Fun fact, I was on the bowling team in high school and was the league president for our team on the base. I thought I could totally school these Veterans on the lanes. I love a good challenge. I thought, who knows I may have some fun? I attended the bowling event and was greeted by two other members of the organization. They were the founding members that later on forge a team to launch a community of over 5,000 people impacting so many lives.

We bowled that day and connected over our service and the willingness to volunteer and give back to our community. We had no idea what was in store. They mentioned they ran on Wednesdays so I met them and we started running down the street with an American flag. Have you ever run while holding one? It's so hard! It was windy and cold. I wasn't even sure what it meant at first. I did it anyway as we forged ahead in the blizzard winter of Buffalo, New York. Nothing was stopping us. Not snow, sleet, hail, wind, negative eleven degrees, absolutely nothing. Even if we were the only ones showing up, we were consistent in our pursuit of growing a community. I didn't realize what an impact that was going to have on my life.

We kept growing as more people started joining us on Wednesdays. We called it "wear the eagle Wednesdays" as this is where eagles fly (run) with the flag around the park. At first, it was all about working out and volunteering. I began to realize I was surrounded by like minded individuals who were trying to live happier and healthier. I found my tribe and I was all for it. Naturally, when they were looking for a Veteran Outreach Director, I applied. I was serving my country, and I loved serving the community as well. I am an extrovert. I was like yes, let me do it! So I organized my first event. It was a 5K around the park just for Veterans, followed by brunch, camaraderie and connection.

The mission of Team Red, White, and Blue (RWB) is to enrich the lives of Veterans through social and physical activity. I loved this mission. I volunteered every day, and became a role model and spokesperson for the organization. By then, I had been single for a very long time, building my independence. In fact I had applied for jobs in Tampa. I was ready to move to a warmer location. What's cool about Team Red, White and Blue is that you can go anywhere and join a chapter. You're never without friends or like minded veterans or community supporters ever again. I loved this idea. I was promoted to the new Veteran Outreach Director of Team Red, White and Blue, and planned my first initiative in my new role. I was excited and scared, but honored to serve our Veteran community.

My knight in shining armor, the man of my dreams named Russ, showed up in a white Cadillac and my life was forever changed. I ran to his car to tell them where to park for the event. I could barely see out of my extra large hoodie that was tied so tight I could barely see out of the tiny peephole. I had six layers of fleece lined clothing and big swish pants that made a lot of noise with every step I took. It was not very sexy.

As we ran around the park he explained a little about his life story. I realized he wasn't local. He had a deep southern accent, was a military man, and huge muscles. He didn't wear a coat, despite the cold. He explained that he had a daughter and was a recruiter in the Army. Some feelings were stirring up inside and I was in a predicament, because this man broke all my rules. Part of my independence was building a tough outer shell. I developed a set of standards and I worked hard to stay true to them. I didn't want to date anyone in the military. I didn't want to be a military spouse. The qualities in his demeanor, kindness, and leadership outshined all my concerns. I thought, first things first, I needed to get this southern man a coat and welcome him into our community. We exchanged cards as recruiters typically do, so we could network and share ideas to help potential recruits choose the best branch of service that they qualify for to meet their plans and goals. Each of our branches had different requirements, so it was helpful to know someone in another branch to bounce questions off of from time to time.

We went to brunch that day after the run in the park. The girls at the restaurant were swooning over him, like fresh meat. I remember calling my friend right away that day. I said "Oh my gosh, do you remember that guy that I always dreamed that I would marry? I think I just met him!" "Get it together Krystal, keep it cool, keep it professional," was my inner chatter. If I told him, he'd think I was crazy. Later on that night, I sent him a welcome text message and gave him ideas of all the different events the team had planned for the week. It was Restaurant Week so everything was $20.14 for most of the nice restaurants around town. He asked me to go to dinner one night that week. OMG a date?!

We were heading to a really nice dinner for our first date. He picked me up in his pearl white Cadillac. It was spotless, shiny, and prestine. I'll never forget the red shirt he wore that showed his muscles and the smell of his fresh cologne and perfectly groomed hair. I wore my white long peacoat with a fur collar, jeans, and a cute blouse. I didn't want to dress up too much. I still had my walls up and I was skeptical. I thought to myself, "ugh Krystal what are you doing? You're moving away, what's the point?" I felt I had to say something. As we were pulling in the parking lot, I froze. I told him, " I'm so sorry, I have to tell you something." He said, "What, are you married or something?" I said, "No, the reason I didn't plan an event for tonight was because I have a telephone job interview tomorrow. It's a job in Tampa, and it's my second interview. It is pretty much a slam dunk. You can turn around now."

    Life is a series of decisions. And in that moment, he looked at me and he said, "Let's still go, we'll share a steak and have a good time." Later that night we joked and laughed as we got to know each other. He said that maybe he'd get to make out with me at the end of the night. I shared I was up for free steak and some good conversation. We talked for hours and laughed and laughed and we shared a steak and veggies. We shared our goals, our values, and trials and tribulations, some of our history, and some of our family stories. We didn't hold back. We had the best night. The next morning I had my job interview and I did okay at best. It was a second job interview over the phone and I thought I had it in the bag. That's what they told me at least. While I waited for the results of the interview, we continued to attend events together every day that week.

    On our third date, I shared my goals for running and he said the magic words, "I've always wanted to run a marathon." I said, "Oh yeah, I'm running one next month. You should join me". He said, "Okay sign me up". He had no idea what he was getting himself into. He thought that if he wanted to date me, he needed to be a runner and he needed to be able to keep up. What a challenge! He was a bodybuilder, but was nursing an injury, so running helped keep his fitness in check instead of lifting.

We trained almost every day together. We went on runs, talked, laughed and ate tons of food. I shared the psychology, nutrition, and everything I had learned about training for a marathon. I had to prepare him to run 26.2 miles in roughly thirty days safely. We were all in and I was going to make sure he was safe, healthy, and strong finishing that race.

A week later, I got a phone call that I didn't get the job. It was the most disappointing, yet happy phone call I've ever had. I was happy I didn't get the job. What a whirlwind. I had been ready to pack up and head to the beaches of Florida to start my life anew. Instead, life shifted on a cold March day in Buffalo. I couldn't wait to call him and tell him that I didn't get the job. He didn't answer and my heart sank. I thought, "Oh gosh, I made a mistake. We totally stayed out too late, I bombed the interview, and now I'm stuck here and he won't answer". It turned out that he was just busy at work. I thought, "Take a chill pill, sheesh Krystal." Love can really send our brain on a wild train of thoughts, insecurities, and doubts to keep us entertained or circling the drain for hours.

He called me back later and celebrated with me, but still was compassionate with the rejection notification, and knew that was something I was wanting to do. He shared that he was really excited to continue to train and finish the marathon. During our last couple training runs, I told him that my celebration after a race is to take a trip. I take a vacation to a beach, an all inclusive resort. He had never been to an all inclusive resort before. We talked and then did some research and he said, "Okay, I'm all in, let's do this". I searched for hours on end as I always do. I had analysis paralysis. God help us, I'm a frugal perfectionist baller on a budget! I searched every search engine and every resort and flight to find the best experience for us to celebrate together, just three months after we met. Holy moly. Was I going to spend a whole week with this man in a hotel room? Oh yes! Everything seemed so natural and we grew as friends, colleagues and really enjoyed each other's company. We shared values of integrity, service, excellence, leadership and also physical activity.

This is where we recognized that purpose, values, social and physical activity is the combination that works.

We went to Cozumel and spent an entire week at the Melia all-inclusive hotel and we had such an amazing time. People thought we had been married for years or we were honeymooners. We had known each other for just three months and people were shocked. The locals would yell, "Oh hey honeymooners!" or "There's Rambo and Barbie." We celebrated the memories of finishing that Buffalo Marathon together carrying the American flag across the finish line hand in hand. We reminisced about the funny water stop experience when he had a calf and quad muscle cramp. I was stopped to bend down and massage his quads. From behind, it looked bad. Really bad. The guys approaching us yelled, "Hey, my legs hurt too, my turn next." We chuckled at all of our memories training, where he would shelter me as I crouched down in between bushes when duty called. We got close real quick. We didn't realize that soon we'd be getting even closer.

We shared some fond memories but also talked about his roommate. There were a couple of times where we witnessed some things that weren't normal and some behaviors that weren't healthy. The roommate liked to drink a lot, would take a lot of medication from various doctors, and had a lot of girls around. At first Russ and I would giggle sometimes as another one went into the back room with him. There were quite a few. We didn't think much of his behavior, as he was young and single. We didn't have concerns until we did. One day, we noticed that a woman was not having fun in his bedroom. We then intervened on a few occasions, beginning to realize that things weren't right. So on this trip, we tried to come up with a plan to get him help and get him to move out. We didn't know when we left for vacation that the roommate's problems would escalate to a mental health crisis.

On the drive home from the airport after our trip, we were on cloud nine. It was like we were coming from our honeymoon. We had a plan for us to spend time together, share memories, and experience life. We planned to be active leaders in Team RWB, growing the community and focusing on our service and our love for social and physical activity. We had found our family and we found a community we loved. We were excited for the future together.

It was a Monday morning. We were both starting brand new positions at work, as we had been promoted at the same time. We were celebrating a new journey; both of us stepping up as new leaders in our roles. We had planned on coffee and a breakfast sandwich before taking on the day. The day quickly shifted as we drove up to the house and we realized something wasn't right. The door was swinging on its hinges. We soon found a trail of garbage, beer cans and bottles, and it smelled horrible. The kitchen counter could not be seen as the dishes were piled high and there were bugs flying everywhere. There were band aids all over the place. And then we walked to the bathroom. It's a scene I will never forget. It reminded me of the movie, Saw. Yeah, that's exactly what it looked like. We were both in shock as we began to clean up.

We hadn't known our welcome home would include having to clean up blood, razor blades, pill bottles, and beer bottles while wondering what the heck had happened there. We both cleaned ourselves up and had to go in to work for our first day in our new jobs. It wasn't until lunchtime when I started to see flashbacks from the scene again. What the heck happened in that bathroom? Where was the roommate? What did he do?

It was time to go into crisis intervention mode. I talked to my boss and said I had to leave. I was excused to help take care of this situation, and most importantly, my own mental and physical health. We went on a quest for answers and questioned the neighbors. We questioned the police. In fact, we had to prove that Russ owned the home. We found out later that the SWAT team had been there for an attempted murder-suicide, and reports showed that the roommate was involved in a love triangle and he wanted out. Thank God he had not been successful in his attempt to end his life nor anyone else's! We had to get him the help that he needed, as we found out that he was brought to the hospital by SWAT and admitted into the psychiatric ward for treatment and observation. He needed long term care, and his family did not live nearby, so we stepped in to assist.

We didn't sleep for a week. I had no previous experience with someone trying to end their life. I had never cleaned up so much blood. I was confused and numb. At night, I would sit for hours with his victims, listening to their stories. We cleaned out the paraphernalia and medication he used to drug these women. We found pictures he had taken while they were passed out from being drugged. He was a very sick man. He got the treatment and care he needed to be rehabilitated.

This experience showed me the importance of teamwork, physical activity, and community, especially during troubling times. Being near death and tragedy can change you, whether you're directly impacted or you know someone that experiences it. It changes your perspective on life, especially when you work to help save people's lives.

As a new couple of just three months, Russ and I learned even more about each other and our leadership styles. We stayed true to our non-negotiables, we had support from our community during this difficult time, and we had support from each other. We still worked out every day, ate healthy, drank water, and slept when we could.

Alternatively, I did not have support at work. I was starting a new job and had someone else's phone during the transition. While I was taking time to help Russ sort things out, a group text message thread was started. The texts said things like "Who does she think she is, taking another day off?" and "They're not married. They just met. Why should she help this person?", "She's good at taking vacations and making spreadsheets. That's about it", "She's helping someone from the Army. That's a different service. That's the Army's job." The list went on. I was floored. I was hurt and upset. They had no idea what I had been going through.

They say be careful what you wish for. They say it's lonely at the top. I started to see how lonely I could be, as I took on this leadership role at work. This also showed me who I could trust, and who was in my circle. It was getting much smaller by the day. I kept my chin up. I did what I needed to do. I communicated with the people that I needed to. My walls went back up. I decided to trust no one; to just do my job and go home.

The more lonely and excluded I felt at work, the more I poured into my health and fitness and my RWB community. I took care of my body and my well being the best I could; having no idea the impact this experience would have on my mental health. To this day, it was probably one of the hardest things we have ever been through. We banded together, cried together, and researched together. I'll never forget the endless hours where we laid on the bed, side by side, with notebooks, looking for online resources, and made several calls to the doctors to get him the care that he needed. There were days where we slept with a baseball bat between us, wondering what could happen next. We kept going like our life depended on it, because it did.

* * *

Crews Beyond Limits Journal Prompts:

1. Recall a situation where you were part of a team that came together to support someone facing adversity. How did your combined efforts make a difference in their journey?
2. Explore the connection between integrity and self-respect. How does living in alignment with your values enhance your sense of self-worth and purpose?
3. Reflect on the role of setbacks and challenges in your journey of hard work. How have these obstacles shaped your character and your approach to pursuing excellence?

5

Changing Lanes

Russ and I finally got the email with official notification of military orders in Harrisburg, Pennsylvania. We were due to leave in roughly two to three months. This is what we had been waiting for. We had an actual date! Everything had been so up in the air and now it was happening! I was moving away from home.

Buffalo is my home. I'm super close with my parents and this is all I knew. Aside from traveling, of course, but I always had a place to go back to that was comfortable. I have had friends there since the fourth grade. I built a community where I volunteered, had friends to go workout, eat, or to happy hour whenever I wanted. I was a regular in many places. I didn't want to give up that sense of home, but I also knew I did not want to live away from Russ. I was torn.

I had to think about what I was going to do with my full time career. I was still under contract, and we were still celebrating our wedding day, getting photo books, and setting up our life as newlyweds. Our first option was for him to move first while I finished up my contract and would move there later. Our second option was that I ask for an exception to end my contract early so I could move away with my husband. We chose option B and when I got the exception approved, things got real. We packed up and drove a few trips back and forth with all of our belongings. Two people combining lives with long standing military careers and tons of personal items was a lot to move! We didn't have much time to go through it all, so we just packed it all up in the U-haul and said "Let's go!"

During our planning, we decided as a couple that my full time career in the military was coming to a close and I'd transition to part time. We were in two different programs and the systems don't accommodate dual military spouses in different branches. It seemed unfair at the time, but this was the best blessing in my life. There's always a silver lining, and it's all in God's timing. Things don't always make sense in the moment but I did not let that stop me. As we moved away from Buffalo, my parents came to help us, tirelessly unloading and setting up and helping us get into our new home together. Everything happened so quickly. I transitioned to a part time position in the military, as a leadership consultant and trainer. I had to travel every three to four weeks back to Buffalo to serve for two days per month. It didn't feel like I had fully left home.

At first, we were just trying to figure out life as a dual military couple navigating travel promotions, competing careers, professional development schools, while traveling for both work and vacations. We were figuring out what married life was like and how we were going to grow our empire together. When we moved, I thought for sure I'd find a job quickly but I was wrong. Since I was a recruiter in the military, I thought for sure finding a recruiting position or an HR position at a local corporation could be an option. That didn't happen either.

During my interviews, I heard comments like: "You've been in the military for how long, sixteen years? You must be so rigid. We're not like the military, there's no way you'll fit in here". "You're a military spouse when you moved here with two months' notice and we want someone with more long term potential. Who's to say you're not going to leave again?" "You're a diversity and inclusion and leadership consultant. You don't look old enough to be able to help anyone with leadership. You're a white woman, what can you teach us about diversity and inclusion? There are really strong men in this company. There's no way you'll be able to connect with them nor teach them anything."

I heard it all. I started taking things off my resume and once again, lowering my standards. Just like that I shrank, feeling smaller and smaller by the day. I just wanted to fit in. I wanted to be at the coffee cooler or in the break room telling jokes. I wanted to be invited to the happy hours. I wanted to belong. I had to travel a lot to retrain in my new military position, while trying to meet new friends when I was home. It's really hard to make adult friends, especially in a small town because there are cliques. They make it very clear what high school and what college you went to define what side of the tracks you are allowed to live on.

I put myself out there by attending networking events and local meet-ups. People would ask me the question I hated to answer; "what do you do?" I never had the right answer. I didn't have a job. I didn't have an identity. No one would hire me. Many times, my response would be, "I just moved here and I serve in the military part time. I'm a military spouse." This dreaded question led to all the stories of family members who served or their near attempts to join the military. Never did the conversation turn into "what are you passionate about and how do you want to create impact?" or "what do you enjoy doing in your spare time?"

Most of my time I spent unpacking boxes, setting up picture frames, trying to create a sense of home while my husband worked endless hours for weeks on end. He got promoted and never took a day off. I guess that's what happens when you marry a type A hard-charger and high performer. I'm such a lucky woman! It's what I love about him. It's never a competition. He wants me to succeed just as much as him! These are things I didn't believe were possible in a healthy relationship. He would come home and ask how my day was and it felt like Groundhog Day every day. I would respond to him with the number of applications for new jobs, getting turned down, or more discrimination and judgment. I was in such despair. I felt like a fragile little girl inside, and I had never felt so alone.

Russ did everything he could to try to keep me somewhat happy. We got a hot tub in the backyard. That helped for a little bit. I loved my hot tub coffee time, spending my mornings out there prior to being a keyboard ninja the rest of the day. Groundhog day: apply for more jobs, get more rejection emails, rinse, and repeat.

He bought us a beautiful bench to put in front of our house so we could watch the sunset, with wine of course. That's what everyone did at five pm daily in our neighborhood. I hoped that one day I would fit in. We would travel every chance we got, as he knows I love the beach. I needed something to look forward to and he would do anything he could to get me to smile again. His support was priceless but I was still so depressed without a full time job.

I received other opportunities right after that to serve full time in the military. It would require me to live in a different state. Nope! Not an option. Although I did consider it briefly because I was in such despair. It seemed like a shiny object and something that could give me my identity back and our household could really use a good paycheck. I declined.

Then, one day, I was on LinkedIn scrolling through posts, attempting to network online with strangers. I had spent six months interviewing and was hopeful that my next purpose and direction would come after serving almost 10 years, full time in the military. Then I saw a message from an angel who said "I want to help the next five transitioning Veterans find their purpose after their service." It jumped off the page at me. "That's me!" I said. I never thought I would be a transitioning Veteran asking for help, but here I was living the dream. After starting

Team Red, White, and Blue, I met and helped several transitioning veterans. I was still serving part time so I didn't think I would be what they were looking for. I didn't know what the term "transitioning veteran" really meant. It was a loss of identity, familiarity, and a loss of feeling of safety. I experienced the loss of purpose, consistency, camaraderie, and loss of power and pride. I had lost it all at once. I had also moved away from my friends, family, and everything else I had ever known for the man of my dreams. Be careful what you wish for. Things aren't always what they seem.

I was able to win a scholarship as one of the five transitioning Veterans. I hopped on a call and I poured my heart and soul out to this woman. She was a saint as she listened to me pouring out my heart. She gave me time and she heard me cry and sob for hours. She asked me some powerful questions. I was depressed without a full time job. I had no paycheck, no energy, and I felt helpless and alone. She quickly asked me, "what do you like to help people with? What do you like to do? What have you been through? What qualifications do you have?" She said, "It sounds like you have some pretty strong core values. And I know that purpose, passion, and your service is important. How are you going to continue to serve? What's your next mission?" I was like, "I don't know. That's what I'm trying to find but no one will hire me. I was a fragile little girl inside. I've never felt so alone. I've cried every day for the last six months. What's wrong with me?"

I spent several hours answering questions and being coached by this saint of a woman named Treasa. I wrote tons of pros and cons lists of all the things that I could imagine doing. All the positions I wanted weren't on Indeed or found by filling out a job application. It didn't exist. It was something that my guidance counselor never talked about. Something I never thought was possible. It was entrepreneurship. Start a business, broke, lonely, and depressed? There's no further fire under my butt than a driving force to change the life and hell I was living in. Game on, let's go! I've done hard things before, so I rolled up my sleeves, and said, "what can I do with what I've got?"

I had started other businesses before, and I had an MBA. My mom and I took an executive level MBA program together in 2009. Yes, I partied with my mom in college! We had an amazing time and became best friends. We studied, we dissected problems, case studies, and created business and marketing plans. We dreamed of beach and ocean celebrations. We also skipped school on a few occasions and had the best happy hours together. She hated public speaking. She would arrive early to class, then spend thirty minutes in the bathroom sick to her stomach about her potential to give a speech or presentation. Alternately, I found that I thrive under pressure. If I knew what I was talking about, then I could show up with thirty seconds to spare and I'd be "on." I had enough practice because I was always trying to maximize every second of every day so I ran into the room like a tornado every time, ready to rock and roll. I guess I'm meant to make a scene wherever I go as I don't blend. I strutted into each class, a unique and petite spectacle, in a fresh pressed suit and stilettos. I showed up no matter what, ready to go! I had practiced my presentation and public speaking skills on the fly for two years straight. My classmates loved me and it was pure entertainment. I worked hard and played harder. I can't believe they put me in charge. But here I am again, living the dream.

We had studied entrepreneurship, with our thesis about starting a business, way before social media was popular. Needless to say, they didn't teach us online marketing. I had to figure it out on my own, grass roots style. I took a free workshop on how to create a landing page with Mailchimp. I started with a few services helping women with their fitness and running. I was so proud of my first business card! I sent the mock up to my mentor, Melissa. She was so proud of me and said she loved it! That was all I needed to hear. She whispered in my ear, "One day, you're going to be a motivational speaker." She's my angel.

Melissa always reminded me of God's faithfulness which reinvigorated the faith in myself. I didn't realize until later that He was speaking to me through her. Melissa has a gift, and anyone that is blessed to know her, knows she will protect and fight for the ones she loves. She taught me the true meaning of leadership, mentorship, and standing up for what you believe in, even when it's the least popular opinion in the room. God, thank you for bringing her to me. She's a powerhouse. I pray to be half the woman she is, in pursuit of my gifts and goals to impact and protect the lives of others.

I would travel home every month to serve my part time military duty. I traveled all over the United States to train and test for my certifications for almost two years. Just after I got accepted into the position, they decided they were going to turn it into a diversity and inclusion program to implement into the military. I had no idea what that was at the time, but I was willing to learn, and open to the opportunity to pilot a program for our nation. I had been in the military for fifteen years. All I knew of the role and promotion that I earned was to mentor and train other soldiers. I was prepared for this. I had traveled for almost two years non-stop getting all my credentials. This would become a true gift of personal development with a foundation of emotional intelligence.

I always thought I was weird and that I never fit in. The story I told myself was that I had too much energy. A lot of people told me I'm "too much", "too happy", or "too peppy". It was a gift from God to learn about emotional intelligence and get certified to train it. This was my chance to learn about who I am to the core. Everything changed after this. I started to realize why I was the way that I was and the energy that I had was not my fault. I'm not weird, I'm just me. I thought about what I could do to impact the world with my uniqueness. As I was learning and on a healing journey, I needed to pay the bills as I got the business off the ground. I needed something flexible to suit my new remote lifestyle.

I applied for a part time job at a hospital and I couldn't believe I was applying for a part time position after being on active duty for almost ten years. I told myself, "this is how it is, and I have to settle for what it is." I felt like that was all I was worthy and capable of. This is where I began to feel the sting of military transition. The job I applied for was a remote position. This was back in 2017, so I wondered, what the heck is a remote position? It intrigued me so I applied. I feel like I only got this job because the head of HR was a military spouse. I had learned really quickly the biases that recruiters have against the military and especially military spouses in small towns where there aren't a lot of transient workers. I don't blame them, it's not their fault. It's only their experience but I was able to change their perceptions. I was the first remote employee the company had ever had. The head of HR said "we weren't looking to hire someone from off the street, but you have exactly what we're looking for. You can work independently, you need the flexibility, and you have the ability and skills to recruit. I feel like you have the "IT" factor and the people skills to do what it takes to hire the best travel nurses and CEOs that we have to offer our company, so we choose you." She's another angel.

    I continued to travel once a month for the military while working at this remote position. I was also trying to coach in person for my business and build a community and make friends in Harrisburg. I still didn't feel like I really owned a business. I asked myself every single day, "who am I?" When I went home to Buffalo, everyone wanted to see me but I had to work all weekend. I always felt pulled in different directions. I was exhausted from the six to seven hour drive one way just to work sixteen hours and then turn back around again to drive back home. I was feeling confused about where home actually was. Was home in Buffalo or Harrisburg? I ran myself ragged for almost five years straight, flying and driving back and forth. Every time I went back to Buffalo, it felt a little less like home. Maybe it was exhaustion or the many times I almost fell asleep at the wheel. Maybe it was the financial strain of barely making ends meet working a part time job at a low wage or not getting paid by the military for my travel back and forth to Buffalo. I constantly felt torn, exhausted, and burned out.

All the travel was also a way of escaping the huge empty home in Harrisburg. It was a three story historic brownstone home, right on the water. It was beautiful but it was lonely. I never realized until this time in my life that someone so busy and surrounded by so many people could feel so alone.

What do I do when I get lonely? I knew I needed social and physical activity. I finally picked myself up and decided to start a Team Red, White, and Blue chapter there in Harrisburg! It was what brought me joy before, so I started running down the street with the American flag again. I started with one step and one run at a time. My husband joined me when he could. We ran The Turkey Trot wearing our Team RWB logo and carried the flag. This got the attention of a few others who joined us after learning about our mission. Then it was me, my husband, and two other people. From there it grew exponentially every week. We grew to hundreds of people, hosted barbecues and parties, volunteered together and went out to dinner. Finally, Harrisburg felt like home.

Shortly after, Russ and I bought a rental property. We fixed it up and flipped it to help several families in the city find their home. We cleaned up garbage, spoiled meat, drug paraphernalia, blood, soiled mattresses, and cockroaches. I know now why some couples who do home renovations together get divorced. It's a tough job, which takes tons of coordination, budgeting, communication, and hard labor. We sweat so much and grew together as a couple and a team. Nothing could stop us, not even scraping up spoiled meat and maggots. There was a lot of tears, laughter, swearing, pizza, and beer.

I'll never forget the day we pulled up a nasty carpet to stain and refinish the hardwood floors in one of the houses. How hard could it be? Our half-broken sander apparently did not apply enough pressure, and only had an hour left till we needed to return it. I hopped on the sander and Russ drove me around, using my 115 pounds as leverage to speed up the process! Yes, there's video footage.

We are entrepreneurs and problem solvers! Our ways of serving and giving back to our community gave us a sense of purpose and helped us establish a sense of normalcy. We worked hard to make the place sparkle and shine. The family was moving in on Christmas Eve, so we added finishing touches like filling the refrigerator with food and decorating a Christmas tree with gift cards and presents for the children, and even for the dog! We love to serve. This was the beginning of building a legacy and our empire.

I still didn't know who I was, but I kept working, traveling, and pushing through. Then, we got orders again just a few months later because my husband got another promotion. I was thinking, "Can you slow down already?" However, he's a high performer and an incredible leader. I'm so proud of him. I was frustrated that we had to move again. I had just barely made a few close friends.

We packed up again and drove down the Pennsylvania Turnpike, moving to Pittsburgh just a short 10 months after moving to Harrisburg. Russ worked even more hours at his new job, and never took a day off, but this time I had a safety net. I had a remote job. That was pretty cool because I had a sense of normalcy and safety, and I was so grateful for this sense of relief. Of course, I had to ask for permission because while it was remote, I was no longer living in the city where the company headquarters were located. Luckily, they understood my situation and allowed me to move, trusting me to take my company laptop and phone to the other side of the state. I found purpose and passion in building a remote national program and found that I was really good at it. I was recognized by my boss and loved the company culture of service and teamwork. I'm forever grateful to them for taking a chance on me. My boss, Nan, has such a kind heart. She went out of her way to value me as a remote team member, and she invited me into her home and to holiday parties. We even did soup swaps! She did her best to make me feel welcome even though I never went into the office. That's true leadership. Like the famous quote by Theodore Roosevelt: "People don't care how much you know until they know how much you care." She is another angel.

I built a national program of business development and recruitment from my new home office. I called it my "command center". I had three laptops, five screens, two mice, and one brain. I was good at what I did. I was proud to make a difference and provide opportunities for nurses all over the country. I hired more military spouses and service members than the company had ever hired before. It brought me so much joy to be able to impact the lives of other Veterans and spouses, as I understood their lifestyle and struggles.

One of the things I learned about moving four times in six years is that people get really comfortable in their hometown. It's not easy to assimilate when you travel for work. When I moved to Pittsburgh, I met an awesome woman named Diana the first day I moved into my new apartment. She was a runner and had so much energy. She was welcoming and happy, just like me. Diana has such a beautiful heart. She welcomed me in and invited me to dinner one night. I poured my heart out to her, telling her what I had been through and the challenges I had been experiencing. God bless her soul. It was kind of like going on a first date telling the person my whole life story. Diana is an angel, too. We're still friends to this day.

My childhood friends back home didn't understand my busy traveling military lifestyle and they questioned what I was doing. They said things like, "I can't keep up with you anymore. I can't possibly follow you. I don't understand why you travel so much. You need to slow down. You've changed so much, why aren't you just happy staying home?" I quickly learned who my true friends were and that I had outgrown some of my longest friendships. I grieved the loss of the friends that I called family for many years. I also learned that it's really hard for people who have never traveled or served in the military to understand what I had been going through. It's not their fault, and I forgive them and miss them terribly. It wasn't their life and it's not their job to understand me. Everyone is on their own road on this journey of life, and it's especially tough leaving friends and family in the rearview mirror. I must keep driving along like my life depends on it, because it does.

* * *

Crews Beyond Limits Journal Prompts:

1. Reflect on the role of teamwork in your own life. How can you actively cultivate an environment of mutual assistance and encouragement within your relationships?
2. Imagine you've hired a coach to guide you through your current challenges. What specific areas would you want to focus on with your coach? How do you envision their support helping you navigate this phase of your life?
3. Reflect on your journey of change and evolving identity. How has your commitment to fitness and wellness impacted your resilience? Imagine writing a letter to your present self from a future version who emerged even stronger from this transformation.

6

Take the Lead

As I packed my bags, my recruiter and the recent graduates gave me advice:

"Don't raise your hand," or "Don't volunteer for anything," or "Don't call yourself out," they say.

They said "Don't wear anything bright - just blend in". I heard these words at the young age of eighteen as I arrived at basic military training. What I didn't realize was that I went there to stand out! I went there to prove myself at 4 ft 11 ¾ inches and 97 pounds. I was a young woman joining the United States Air Force in May 2002, just eight months after 9/11. Twenty one years later, I found myself still trying to blend in so I could belong.

They say things like "don't break your military bearing" or "check your feelings at the door". There were also demeaning comments like "being in the military, you'll never get a man because you're too strong" or "you better shave your arms, they're too hairy. Maybe then someone will like you" or "you're not like us, you belong in the office and the kitchen".

They just don't get it. I spent time in construction and computer engineering in the military. I became one of the guys at work in many ways, but something was always missing. I was never invited to the parties, happy hours, or the closed door meetings. I stood out too much. I was too pretty, too energetic, and of course, I was friendly. I was just trying to fit in, but the more different I was, the more excluded I felt. Instead of fitting in, I stood out like a unicorn in a herd of sea lions. Instead of being fully included, I heard things like:

"What would their wife say? What would the other female soldiers say?"

"She couldn't possibly be able to manage our project. What does she think she knows?"

"Who does she think she is? I've been in the military for over 30 years - what is she gonna teach me?"

"There's no way you can coach me"

"Does she think she is a life coach or something? How embarrassing."

Then one day, my boss invited me to speak to over seven hundred of my coworkers in an auditorium. Gulp. I was thinking, "Wow this is my chance for them to see what I really do and the value I bring!" I was excited but nervous. We had just faced a shutdown and a change in our mission. Many people were going to need to make major career changes but did not understand the process. They were afraid of losing their jobs, their traditions, and their identity. It was at this moment I realized I could be an advocate for change and help bridge the gap for the future. I knew I could help people with their lives, their families, their finances, and their education. My previous career experience at HSBC as a licensed broker had given me the skills to assist with the transition. I'm trained to ask some powerful questions like, "How are you going to keep benefits?

What would your wife/husband think? What's really going on here and how can we fix this? Is there another job that will suit you? How can you continue to serve, do what you love, and feel fulfilled in your position? I realized that I was a life and career coach. I was guiding my colleagues to look at the bigger picture and create a roadmap for a brighter future, career, and life.

As I confidently approach the microphone, I looked at the crowd of hundreds of people. I was proud and honored to share my passion and purpose during this challenging season of change.

I had helped many people privately with their finances, their family, their career, and the impact that their decisions had on their life. People shared things with me that only their closest friends and colleagues knew. I kept our conversations confidential, even when others questioned me, looking for information. It was difficult. I had helped so many people, but no one knew the depths of the work that was done behind closed doors. So when I took that stage, it was my chance to share my passion about the impact that I was making in serving others.

I explained with confidence, "I help you handle all of your life situations. We will get clear on your core values and address all aspects of your life: your finances, your relationship with your family, your personal and professional development, your career, your goals and dreams, your leisure, and even your spiritual life. I am creating a roadmap that will launch your career to the next level." Then these words came out of my mouth unplanned: "I'm a life coach, and I'm here in your corner, no matter what." I had no idea what a life coach was but it felt so right and filled me with pride. Many people that I had already helped were in the audience listening intently. They were cheering me on because they knew the value of the help I could provide.

That speech was only about ten minutes long but I was on top of the world for the rest of the day and then some! As I walked back to my office, I heard whispers in the hallways. "Who does she think she is? She thinks she's some sort of life coach? She's not qualified to say that. She's so young. What does she know about life? How could she help people with her finances?"

While many people had an opinion on the work I was doing, only a few curious individuals actually came to talk to me about it. Later that day, someone told me who was making all these comments and starting the whisper train - funny thing was, it was another woman. Go figure! She actually had no idea who I was and didn't realize the ways in which her comments influenced my life forever.

Have you ever judged someone before ever having a conversation with them? Congratulations, you're human! Me too. As I have grown, I have found that when I have this instinct, I need to get curious and ask more questions. If you can slow down your thinking, it will change the way you speak.

    Spend five minutes with the person before you make your judgment. The more data and context you have, the more accurate your opinion will be. This process can bring more positive outcomes in relationships and in life.

I knew I was doing the right thing. I was meant to stand out. I was meant to be the first life coach that anyone knew. I was meant to step on that stage and share my message in service. I was meant to step into that arena. The people that I had already coached knew how I had carried the empathy, the compassion, the love, the research, the support, the challenging conversations, the tears, the pain, the anger, and the frustration for years.

Sometimes when you start something new, you feel like you lose the previous experience and identity you have developed. If you capitalize on your strengths and experience as a foundation it all comes together. I did what I could with the skills I had at the time. I went all in, and strived for integrity, service, and excellence every single day. When I took the stage I explained the educational benefits process for changing careers, the medical requirements and process they would have to go through. I was the only one that could have this conversation.

Serious conversations are not easy to have. It's not easy to open up and be vulnerable about your body, your finances, your heart, your mind, your family, your faith, or your dreams and goals. I shared my own vulnerable moments by telling them my stories. I believed in them. I did whatever I could to help ease their pain through their transition. I tried to help them make powerful decisions. I know I made a difference but what I learned was that I didn't need to stand out. I didn't need validation from the people who didn't come to me. If they had, they would have felt the love, compassion, and support I offer. They would know that I meet them where they're at, without judgment. What's ironic is that later, some of them did ask for my help. This is the ultimate test of integrity. How do you let go of hurt and anger, in order to help them become more successful? I needed to put my own judgment aside. I still helped them with a smile. Some of them commented, "Wow, you are different than I expected. The things they say aren't true at all. I'm so glad I came today. Thank you for helping me and my family".

Back in 2010, life coaching wasn't a thing many people knew about. Facebook had just put MySpace out of business. Many people were familiar with the concept of mentors, therapists, and counselors, but not life coaches. I was the first one many people had encountered. Some people would make negative comments until they needed something.

Then I saw the other side of them. When they crossed the threshold into my office, the mask they wore in public to fit in was taken off. All of the judgment and bias dropped away. They had to be vulnerable in order to survive and thrive in their career. Some people told me things that they have never told anyone else, things that they could never tell their supervisor. I locked everything up like a vault, and held their stories close. They knew they could trust me, even when I did not feel I could trust them.

Sometimes their supervisors would come to me, wanting to fire or reprimand them. Sometimes they just needed to vent about how disappointed they were in how their high-performing employee had disengaged. I was there for them too. I heard it all, from both sides. I was stuck in the messy middle. What they needed was to be asked the deep questions - to talk about values, dreams, emotions, and impact. They needed to receive the love and support they craved. We all just want to be heard, feel valued, trusted, and understood. This is the feeling of belonging. The biggest reasons for relationship conflict are miscommunication and misunderstanding.

Where in your relationships are you experiencing conflict or static? Perhaps a conversation is necessary. Commit to a dialog before you judge. Spend five minutes with that person - say, "let's grab a coffee." Pull up a couch or a barstool, or go for a walk. It's not another person's job to understand the personal journey you are on. We can all be a little more open, honest, and empathetic. Commit to having a dialog. Open the door.

I learned the power of courageous confidence to tackle difficult situations in these challenging moments. Sometimes it's scary to have difficult conversations, and do things that aren't popular or lead to being misunderstood. It never gets easier, you get stronger. Continue to be uniquely you and no one else. Stay true to your purpose, your passion, and the people you serve, no matter what. Have integrity and give selfless service. Do everything with excellence like your life depends on it, because it does.

***

Crews Beyond Limits Journal Prompts:

1. Reflect on a time when you felt misunderstood or underestimated in your personal journey. How did that experience shape your perspective on the importance of empathy? Consider how opening up dialogues and practicing openness can foster greater understanding and connection among people. Write about a situation where you can commit to having a meaningful conversation with someone, promoting empathy and connection.
2. Think about a time when you felt the pressure to conform or be someone you're not. How did this experience impact your sense of authenticity and purpose? Reflect on the ways in which staying true to yourself allows you to serve others more effectively. Write about how you can continue to embrace your uniqueness and authenticity while serving the people who resonate with your purpose.
3. Consider a recent instance when you had to make a decision that required integrity and selfless service. How did your commitment to these values guide your actions? Reflect on a specific area of your life where you can apply the principle of doing everything with excellence. Write about how approaching each task with dedication and excellence is not just a choice, but a reflection of your life's purpose.

7

Heartbreak Hill

It was 2005, and I was waiting and ready. When the lights turned on, it was game time. The walk through the tunnel seemed to take forever as my heart was beating out of my chest. Seventy Thousand (mostly drunk) fans screamed as I walked out onto the field. What a rush! Then the self-doubt crept in and I was terrified. What if I screwed up? What if I forgot my moves? Did I eat enough? What if I'm too cold? Did I put enough hand warmers on? Who will I see in the stands? Do I have lipstick on my teeth? Is my hair out of sorts? Everyone was watching. They were always watching.

Being an NFL cheerleader was such an amazing experience. My aunt was a cheerleader and she showed me what was possible. I was living a legacy. I had made it to the NFL! Five hundred women auditioned with me. Only thirty eight were selected to be dancers on the field. I had to try out again every week to remain on the team. We had weekly physique evaluations, a solo performance, and a group performance of choreography we had learned only the day before. My moves had to be sharp, and my hair and makeup had to be perfect. I had to be on at all times, and I loved every minute of it.

In the fall, I was selected to do a runway show for the Spirit Halloween store. It was October 31st, and I was the last person to pick up my costume. I was running myself ragged; going to school full time, working part time, and then rushing to cheer practice. I was checking in and out of the gym, getting spray tans, and somewhere trying to fit in eating some food. I was barely sleeping. Commuting back and forth to Buffalo during blizzards wasn't easy either. I chose a witch costume. I had to buy black stiletto shoes to wear with it, as I don't wear a lot of black typically. (Although I can be a witch if I need to...it's the little ones you gotta watch out for, you know! But that's for my next series.)

I strutted my stuff at the Halloween runway show in cheap Payless black stiletto heels. I woke up on November 1, 2005 and my feet hurt. I was shocked to see that my right baby toe was bright red and bigger than my big toe. Comfort over fashion was not an option here. It hurt for days before I finally went to the doctor. They said, "You have an ingrown toenail. Stop wearing those shoes. Stop working out so much. You need to slow down anyways. Put your feet up for a while and you'll be fine." So I did just that. In the middle of a blizzard, I wore flip flops because I couldn't put on a shoe.

A few weeks later my right knee started hurting. It was achy and it burned on the inside with no visible injury. About a week later, my left knee began hurting too. Then the pain extended to my right shoulder, then from my left shoulder to my jaw. It was locked up for three months, and I had to eat out of a straw. Within weeks, my entire body shut down. I was only 22 years old, and I could no longer walk. I was devastated. I went to the doctor and he told me the same thing the others had; "You're doing too much. You need to slow down. You just need rest". This was a cycle repeated many times.

My doctors told me I had to wait two to three months to be able to see a specialist for testing. I couldn't walk. I was an NFL cheerleader. I was in school full time and I had to work. "I don't have time for this!" I thought. I was frustrated, overwhelmed, and in so much pain.

I was in the senior year of my undergrad degree at Buffalo State College. I was in a financial securities class, sitting front and center, trying to pay attention and learn about the stock market even with everything else going on in my life. I frequently took pages of notes for my partner, who sat next to me. She shared her struggles with Lupus - her invisible illness - with me. She was constantly going to the doctor, and though she didn't even look like she was in pain, she experienced it constantly. Thank God she talked to me. She was one of my angels. I helped catch her up every time she would miss a class.

After months of doors being closed in my face, confusion over not being able to walk, and being in massive amounts of pain, I told my class partner what I was going through. I said, "I think this sounds a bit like what you've experienced. Can you tell me more about your condition?" At this time, they had no idea what was wrong with me. Rheumatoid arthritis (or arthritis of any kind at that matter) was not on the radar. I was twenty-two years old, so I wasn't considered pediatric or geriatric. Talking to her was the first time I realized how different I really was. She said "Well, let me ask my doctor." He called me at 8 o'clock that night (a Friday night.) He said, "Your friend was in my office earlier and told me a little bit about your story. I'll get you in next week. I'm not taking any new patients but for you, I will. I'll see you then." He was another angel.

This led down a road of what felt like endless amounts of testing and medication. Ultimately, we figured out I had a very rare form of Rheumatoid arthritis. And even that was weird for the doctors. I spent six months in a wheelchair. They poked and prodded at me for months until they found a special cocktail that allowed me to walk with minimal pain. The medicine regimen was an almost lethal mixture - a chemotherapy pill and a steroid injection that had to be refrigerated. I had to inject it by needle into my quads and my abdomen every other day. I also had to take more supplements and vitamins to offset the ulcers that the medicine was burning inside my body. I had an AM/PM pill box that was bigger than my head. This daily routine was the combination of treatments that enabled me to move. I could not put my two feet down from the bed onto the floor because my joints were so stiff and painful. Each day, I had to fall out of bed and crawl for a little bit before I was able to walk. The doctors said this would be like this for the rest of my life. I was in shock while hearing this heartbreaking news.

The next step was taking my medical documentation into work at the Air Force Base. Immediately they said, "this medication is disqualifying. We have to separate you from the military, your career is over." At this point, the doctors had already told me I would never be able to run again, and that I would have to be on all of this medication for the rest of my life. I could no longer be an NFL cheerleader. I was so out of shape and had gained weight from not moving and the endless amounts of steroids and medication. I grew sideways in that wheelchair, gaining so much weight and feeling helpless. There was no way the NFL would accept me back. I assembled a binder filled with documentation on my medication, doctor's notes, follow ups, and timelines to try to prove that I was still able to serve despite my condition, but they said no. "But I am an athlete," I thought, "This doesn't seem right."

Thankfully, the military medical review process is pretty long, and it requires a lot of paperwork, signatures, and reviewing in multiple layers. As I waited for the verdict that would end my career, one night I found myself being rushed to the hospital. My entire leg swelled, itching and stressed with pain. It turns out I had so much joint fluid that it filled my entire left leg, from my quad and groin area all the way down to my ankles. It was incredibly painful. The doctor extracted bright orange joint fluid out of my leg with a huge needle. It was ugly. The ER nurse was an angel. As she looked at me, she said, "You look familiar. You work at the base, don't you?" I said, "Yes I do." She said, "You're that crazy runner girl, aren't you?" I said with a sad smirk, "Yep," even though I knew that identity was long gone. She said, "You're an athlete. This doesn't seem right." I agreed. Finally, someone gets me! She listened to my story. She said, "Maybe there's another way. Let's figure this out." So we worked together to understand the rules and regulations for remaining active in the Air Force. I learned to understand more about inflammation. This angel gave me hope that there was another way to heal my body and maybe I could continue to serve. So, I worked with my doctors for an entire year as they made me a test subject for medication, injections, and steroids. I read "Rheumatoid Arthritis For Dummies". I studied the power of nutrition, anti-inflammatory diets, movement and soon learned about mental health's effects on physical health. Looking back, I realize that this was the first time I experienced depression and loneliness. This is when I recognized that I was in a toxic relationship with my boyfriend at the time, who lived in my house. But even worse, I was in a toxic relationship with myself and my health. I was burned out - emotionally, physically, spiritually, financially. I had kept going on past my breaking point, and my nervous system was stuck.

    After working with my doctors for an entire year, I was able to get off all the medication. I started with crawling, until my joints were loose enough to walk. I walked when I could to keep moving. I was so grateful to be able to move. "I get to move" was my mantra. Then I started jogging - one light post at a time, one stop sign at a time, one block at a time, one mile at a time, one 5k at a time, one 10k at a time, one half marathon at a time, then one marathon at a time. At first, I was running away to escape the pain from the toxic relationship that I had with myself. I was running to get out of the house, to escape the depression and loneliness. I loved the feeling of running - I was addicted. I felt so free and gained a sense of accomplishment. The only thought on repeat in my head was, "I'm not in that wheelchair anymore." I'll never forget shopping in Value City for my first couch in a wheelchair, barely being able to move my body from the wheelchair to the couch. That's window shopping at its finest. I kept running because I knew that my life depended on it. The impact that running has had on my mental health and my physical health is undeniable. It's my time, it's my meditation, it's my sanity. As of the date of writing this book, I have run twenty six marathons and a fifty mile ultra marathon race. I don't take ibuprofen or any medication for my Rheumatoid Arthritis, an autoimmune condition that is in remission. My doctors call me a freak of nature to this day. They told me I'd be on endless amounts of medication for the rest of my life. I was going to prove them wrong. After a few years, I continued to improve my run times, and was able to have a fast enough time to qualify and run for Boston, New York, Chicago and Berlin. I thought, "I got this – I'm on a mission!" I decided I was going to run all six World Marathon Major marathons. I set a goal to get the medal that only 8,000 people in the entire world have been able to accomplish. I will complete all six, after being in a wheelchair. No matter what. No matter how long it takes. The doctors told me I would never be an athlete again. I've vowed to prove them wrong, to "crews beyond limits." This is where this phrase was born. Many times people and society place limitations on us, telling us what we cannot or should not do. We have a choice to listen to those voices or find another way, and defy the odds, the generational patterns, and most importantly, forget about the opinions of others.

Over the years, as I continued to try to build my business and my running career, I knew something still wasn't right. With all the moves, I still felt lonely. My husband was always working and I was a lonely entrepreneur. Before the global pandemic of COVID-19 in 2020, I was running an online business and no one knew what the heck it was all about. At first, I wasn't very successful. I had no idea what I was doing or how to market myself online. I taught myself a lot, and used Youtube University. I took a few free workshops to gain some more skills, while traveling back and forth for the military and working a government contract for leadership consulting. "How's your little business?" people in my life would ask. "Once you get a real job…" they would say. I had a steady flow of job applications, contacts, and LinkedIn requests sent to me from friends and family, encouraging me to apply. They wanted the best for me, however, I wanted something more. I was a diversity and inclusion consultant before this civil unrest. I was a white woman facilitating inclusive leadership courses nationwide. I wanted so bad to fit in and to belong. I just wanted to be seen for the value and experience I bring to the table. I felt like a little girl again, trying to get attention. I was determined to prove them wrong too.

Then I learned the power of the brain - how stress and trauma can manifest itself in your body physically, and noticed a mole popped up on my left forearm. It scabbed up, flaked over, then came back again. This was odd. The first time I noticed it, I was in training for the military and was being coached by Apryl, who was another angel. She spent hours and hours, sometimes till four am as I cried, vented, and tried to make sense of my purpose in life. I was harboring the grief and stress of losing friends and how their opinions were taking over my life, on top of moving away from home. A scab on my arm meant nothing to me when compared to the scabs that were being ripped open in my heart and the shackles that were on my feet from the opinions of others. I felt so stuck, like I was in quicksand, descending into a sinking hole.

When I returned home, after resting my body and brain from my emotional hangover, I googled, "What is a mole on your arm that scabs up?" What came back was the word I never wanted to hear - cancer. It took me a little while to actually call the doctor because I was so scared and confused. I thought, "There's no way it's cancer. Maybe it's nothing. Maybe I just got a new beauty mark" However, this one looked a little bit different. It was much darker than the other beauty marks all over my body. I thought, "It's totally natural. My beautiful mom has beauty marks all over her." I didn't think this was any different until it flaked over a third time. "Well, this isn't good," I thought. I finally called the doctor and they said I needed to see a dermatologist. Then they quickly told me that it was going to be a two month wait to be seen. Two months?! My heart sank. I've already waited two months to be able to get the courage to call! Every single day I looked at that web page I found through google and it said that skin cancer is the most aggressive form of cancer. It made it sound like I basically had six months to live and I had to wait two months to be seen!

Once I was finally in for my appointment they recommended emergency surgery. "Oh, and by the way, you have one on your leg that needs to be removed as well." The surgery was in October, two months later.

I know now that the fear of death changed me forever. My life flashed before my eyes. Everything I wanted to do, every dream I had, and every regret flooded my brain. I was fearful of what the future would bring. I thought of my family and friends, and how I would not have the life that I desire.

Once again, I was in recovery mode. I had incisions on my arm and leg, and they both looked like soft, stuffed sausages. I'm a small human and they took huge chunks out of my arm and leg, and looked like a shark bite. A shark bite would have been a cooler story. I couldn't work out for six months and once again, I was in the crawl phase. Once again, I was starting in the fetal position mentally, physically, spiritually, emotionally. Once again, I had to learn and understand what was happening in my body. I had to make a choice: was I going to tap out or keep going? I almost quit my business. I thought, "All right, I've had enough. It's time to go get a real job. Things aren't working out. And clearly I need help."

Then I heard about a conference for female Veteran and military spouse entrepreneurs. I made a deal with myself. I decided to get back up, and so I registered. At this conference, I set goals for my life and my business. I got hopeful and excited about the future again. I set new standards and non-negotiables for my life. And I started to feel hopeful for the future of my business, when I was sinking in despair just weeks before. After the conference, I knew I needed to make a change. I needed a network of support, of other entrepreneurs struggling, trying to crawl and walk in entrepreneurship. I knew that in order for me to put myself in the game, I needed to start taking massive action.

Up until this point, I was still hiding, shrinking, and so afraid to be visible. Online, I would share other people's quotes, memes and jokes because I thought that was what happened in online business. I learned that in order to go from running to sprinting in business, I needed to be a leader. I needed to forge ahead. I needed to get out from behind the curtain. I needed to go down the deep dark tunnel, out to where all the lights are, where everyone's looking at you, waiting for you to show up, so you can help them.

Being courageously confident in these moments helped me as I stepped into the role-model mindset. It was time for me to be a leader. I realized that I can help others shorten their period of self doubt and overwhelm, by sharing my knowledge. I made a vow to myself and God to create a legacy. I am a role model. I am a thought leader. I also realized there is a ripple effect to me showing up. I learned that if I don't show up, I'm robbing all the people that are suffering from abuse, toxic relationships, identity crisis, cancer, disability discrimination, depression and loneliness. I am robbing them of the opportunity to heal, to listen to my story. I vowed to keep showing up no matter what. Like my life depends on it. Because it does.

* * *

Crews Beyond Limits Journal Prompts:

1. Visualize a scenario where you're stepping into the spotlight with unwavering self-assuredness. What message or story do you want to share with the world? How can you make this visualization a reality in your life?
2. Think about a cause, topic, or idea that you're passionate about. How can you use your voice to contribute positively to this area? What actions can you take to ensure your voice is heard and valued?
3. Reflect on a time in your life when you encountered a significant setback, whether it was due to illness, injury, or unexpected career challenges. What were the emotions and thoughts that arose during that time? Now, imagine you're writing a letter to your past self from the vantage point of your present moment. Share the lessons you've learned, the resilience you've discovered, and the growth that has emerged from that setback. How can these insights guide you as you navigate your current situation? Consider the potential for transformation, reinvention, and newfound strength as you continue forward on your journey.

8

The Turning Point

In order to step into the "Next Level" version of you, you have to have "Next Level" confidence - and that's scary! You think: Do I trust myself? Do I trust others? As you go after your dreams and goals, the flood of emotions rushes in. The fear creeps in. When this happens, it's easy to retreat. It's natural for the brain to want to stay comfortable. It's normal to search for the quickest, most efficient way from point A to point B. The secret sauce to success is to honor the journey. It's about becoming who you are while you pursue success.

The S.U.C.C.E.S.S. model is an acronym that I've been using for years. An acronym is pretty cute and easy to remember. It's really hard to follow the principles without a tactical roadmap. That's what I'm going to give you here.

- S - See your goal
- U - Understand the obstacles
- C - Create a positive mental picture
- C - Clear your mind of self doubt
- E - Embrace the challenge
- S - Stay on track
- S - Show the world you can do it

I've always loved this word and this acronym makes it even better. Success looks really pretty at the top. When we are around successful people or see them on the internet, it's easy to feel like we're not good enough, fit enough, pretty enough or have enough followers. It's easy to decide we shouldn't move forward because we compare ourselves and feel unworthy. The mountain is steep and it takes a lot of steps to get there. Most successful people don't share all of those steps - their messy middle.

I used to avoid sharing my journey for fear of judgment, fear of other people's opinions, and the fear of being visible. I didn't want to be seen as weak. I created my secret sauce to use in seasons of change, during struggles and adversity. When experiencing illness, injury and everything in between, I realized that I needed to have trust and confidence in myself. I needed to believe that I would figure it out like my life depends on it, because it does.

My secret sauce is just like my grandma's Sicilian pasta sauce recipe. It is sweet and spice and everything nice. It requires some TLC and a combination of things that make it taste good. In seasons of change and challenges, and going after big, audacious, bodacious goals, I needed confidence. I also needed courage. I wasn't very good at math in school, but I figured out this equation:

Confidence + Courage = Results

You have to put the two together. Yes, it's scary. There's fear - but being courageously confident with consistency breeds massive results. It can have positive, neutral, or negative results. Either way, being courageous and confident means you're ready for results, no matter what the outcome. In the end, there's always a lesson. And the biggest lesson is that results won't come if you don't try. It all starts with you; knowing who you are to the core (your posture, your energy, and how you walk into a room). It matters how you look, how you dress, how you take care of yourself, and the shoes that you wear. My grandmother always told me you can tell a lot about a person by how clean their shoes are - so growing up, we always had clean, white shoes. Recognizing that your energy arrives before you do has been one of the most impactful lessons I have ever learned.

I had to learn to be courageously confident before I believed I was confident. I had to "fake it till I make it". Basically, it is a "baptism by fire". You just get to get in there and do it. The worry and the fear and the "what if's?" suddenly creeped in as I started my Leadership consulting company in June of 2020, just three months into the COVID-19 Pandemic. The country was already hurting and had gone through a divisive time of civil unrest and people needed help.

I had been trained and certified in Diversity Equality and Inclusion (DEI) since 2017. I had been working in the DEI space for three years, building inclusive teams and being a leadership consultant for multimillion dollar projects across the country. As I grew my experience, I saw the impact I was making on teams, corporations, and leaders all across the country. I began to grow in my confidence as a leader, a coach, a mentor and a role model. My phone and email rang with opportunities to offer training at corporations all over the country, but was also faced with a ton of skepticism, criticism and adversity.

Another part of leadership and knowing who you are is knowing your unique personality and what you bring to the table. Are you an extrovert? Are you super organized? Are you a problem solver who loves science and puzzles? Do you love a good challenge and adventure? Do you value harmony and love? How do you communicate? What are your love languages? How do you receive information and how do you learn? What are your core values? Why is it that you do what you do?

I loved learning about psychology and human behavior, and I loved to help others in their self discovery journey. I know that I'm good at what I do and know that I'm meant to be a leader in this space. Truthfully, I was shaken by people's perceptions of the work I did. The most essential human needs are to feel heard, valued, understood, and to feel a sense of belonging. I didn't feel any of this during this period of time. After doing some internal work, I realized that diversity is more than race and gender, and I was more than qualified to start a consulting firm. I was courageously confident and I went for it.

During this time, I was running my fitness business as a health and wellness coach. Once again, people's perceptions of what I did had me torn. How do I introduce myself? Who am I to the core? Am I a fitness coach? Am I a leadership coach and consultant? How can I put this all together? So many people told me I needed to keep it separate and choose one identity over the other. I listened to the advice of others, and I spent nine months rebranding a business plan and website, investing thousands of dollars.

I partnered with people who gave me hope but never truly bought into my vision. It's not their fault. It's not their vision, it was mine. And I'm going after it. Insert Crews Beyond Limits mentality. There I was again, the lonely running down the sidewalk with a flag. I had a makeshift brand and website, and was bleeding from debt. I didn't give up.

I recognized very quickly how my energy dips when other people don't understand me, when I'm around the wrong people, and when I feel out of alignment with my purpose. I knew I needed to figure out a recipe, so I didn't back down. I vowed to be unstoppable, unshakeable, and unbreakable. I knew that part of this was that I needed to fuel my body properly. I needed to hydrate and I needed to move my body, no matter what. I also needed to be around people who aligned with my values. Down to the core, I needed to know who was on my team and who was not. This requires trust and confidence in other people as well.

Once I developed a set of standards, as I knew this would help me make decisions. This would be part of the recipe. Here are my recommendations for you: Show up with a positive attitude. Trust yourself, and know that you will figure it out, even if you have no idea what you're getting yourself into. Know who you are to the core, your essential values, your personality traits, the things that make you unique. Only YOU have what it takes to do what you do. You are uniquely you, no one else. The only competition is you. How are you going to fuel yourself to take charge, take the leap, or to climb the mountain of success?

It starts with making a powerful decision. Get back to the basics. Deciding is power and growth is not comfortable. It's not supposed to be. Similar to exercise, it never gets easier, you just get stronger. We get stronger by showing up, no matter what – like your life depends on it, because it does.

To get started, you will need to decide the following:

Who are you to the core? How do you introduce yourself and who do you show up for to make a difference in the world? I highly recommend not introducing yourself as your title anymore. Introduce yourself with strong, confident posture, leading with your core values, and with courageous confidence about the mission you're on and the legacy you want to create.

For example, here's mine:

I'm on a mission to help empower every woman on the planet to have courageous confidence by putting themselves and their health first for just thirty four minutes a day, so they can reduce the stress and overwhelm of life and live a more fulfilling life. Who doesn't want that?

* * *

Crews Beyond Limits Journal Prompts:

1. As you conclude this chapter, take a moment to ponder your core values. What fundamental principles guide your decisions and actions? How have they evolved throughout this experience, and how do they shape your path forward?
2. As you step into the next chapter of your life, consider the new way you'd like to introduce yourself to the world. How can you capture the essence of your growth and transformation in a few impactful words? Write down your refreshed introduction, reflecting the person you've become.
3. Contemplate the legacy and impact you aspire to leave behind. Imagine yourself looking back from the future. What mark do you want to leave on the lives of those you've touched? How can you shape your actions today to ensure that legacy becomes reality?

9

Confidence Unleashed

We all know we can't predict the future, no matter how much we wish we could! If you don't have a goal, plan, or target, you're just going to float through life untethered. Other people are going to start taking over your schedule, your priorities, and ultimately, your happiness. Your life and your body is like a vehicle, and the goal is to be in the driver's seat, in control. If you're not following the courageous confidence model, someone else might end up taking the wheel.

I speak to people every day who are no longer in the driver's seat of their life, who feel unable to take the wheel and steer. Does this sound familiar? Are you in the back seat watching the scenery out the window while other people's opinions and priorities are taking over? Many servant leaders are perfectionists and people pleasers. It's so easy for our dreams and goals to take a backseat or even end up in the trunk, cast aside and forgotten. Worse, perhaps they're like the "Just Married" beer cans tied on with strings, making a faint noise behind you, as you're holding on for dear life to the bumper by a thread.

That was me, holding on for dear life, trying to grow an online business in 2017. I was constantly asking myself, "Who do I think I am?" I was so worried about what other people would say and think about my decisions. I let their opinions or fears for me stifle my progress. I was letting them sit in the driver's seat and steer my car. For a few years, I was on the sidelines - hiding, shrinking, and making myself small. I was sitting back, watching everyone else succeed. I was thinking, "There's no way I can do what they do!" This was a story that played on repeat in my head for almost two years straight. I needed to no longer be the victim in my story. It was time to step up, brush off the dirt, and start doing things differently if I wanted to change the outcome. The stories we tell ourselves, about ourselves, shape our beliefs. They influence the decisions we make. In order to stop the broken record, I got honest with myself and asked myself some powerful questions.

In 2017, after six months without a job, broke, scared, and lonely while transitioning from fulltime to part time military service, I began to ask myself:

What do I desire for my life?
  What can I do with what I've got?
  What is freedom?
  If I want to start a business, what's going to be required of that?
  How do I need to show up?
  What are my values?
  What is my mission?
  What is my vision?

The responses to these questions were clear and evident in my heart. I knew I needed to take meaningful action and I needed to start right then. I realized I needed to change the standards for my life and decide on my daily non-negotiables. I also learned that I needed a rinse and repeat model that was clear, courageous, and confident. My goal and mission focus was to empower every woman on the planet to put themselves and their health first, for just thirty four minutes per day. I wasn't going to be able to do that without getting myself out there and being visible. I rolled up my sleeves and got to work! I studied what other business owners did. They hired business coaches. Apparently, it helps immensely when you have a good coach in your corner to ignite your fire, challenge you, and in turn, change your life.

I stopped comparing myself to people who had paved the way before me. I flipped the script in my head, choosing to see them as someone to learn from instead. This is where the real work began. My first business coach told me that I needed to go live on social media - to post my pictures and videos with my own thoughts. I felt myself crawling inside my skin. I was so scared. Military life conditioned me and taught me to stay under the radar. Don't stand out. Don't call attention to yourself.

In order to make a change, I needed to get clear on my "why" - who was I showing up for? I needed to understand what I needed to show up confidently. Who did I want to become? More importantly, who or what was getting in the way, and how would I get past those obstacles? I created some rules for myself. With a set of standards for my life, there would be no confusion. No throwing in the towel. No quitting. It's never an option. I needed a system, structure, and discipline in order to propel my growth, progress, and momentum.

I needed to "own it", as my coach would say. My rules were simple. I highly recommend you create a set of rules and standards for your life too. Here's mine to give you some ideas:

1. Show up, no matter what. Especially when it's hard or you don't want to.
2. Work hard. Deliver excellence and give yourself grace that each day probably will look different.
3. Don't quit. The pain of failure and regret sucks. I prefer the pain of endurance.
4. Crews Beyond Limits - you can grow beyond the limits that are in front of you and most importantly the limits between your ears by managing your self talk.
5. Have fun! We don't need to take ourselves too seriously.

Following these rules helped me to visualize: who do I need to become? What are my standards and non-negotiables? What does my dream day look like?

I wrote a letter to myself to help me develop a vision of what I wanted my life to be and to take action on that vision. That letter would forever change the game for me. Here is what I wrote:

Hey there, beautiful,

No one is coming to save you. You need to be courageously confident and show up no matter what. You need to be deliberate in your dreams and find balance in the eight pillars of your life. You need to set intentions and goals in the following areas: health and fitness, career, personal growth, spirituality, relationships, social and leisure, quality of life, and your finances. Get it together. You need to create a dream day ritual. What do you desire?

Then I wrote down my dream which went like this:

I wake up every morning at 5am excited to take on the day.

I give some love to my husband and immediately get to a workout. I am the best wife ever.

I do not work or check email until after my workout, have my coffee, and complete my journaling, meditation, and prayer.

I have a team who loves what they do, and they live the brand.

I have a thriving business and people are shouting from the rooftops, "what a movement"!

There are more happy and healthy people in this world as a result of me showing up.

I have loving, close and trustworthy friends that I can confide in.

I travel to speak on stages and I am constantly being asked to share my message.

I eat clean, practice flexible dieting, and I have a toned body.

I travel to beaches quarterly to recenter, reflect, and re-energize.

I will live 10 steps from the ocean someday.

And I write all of these statements down in my journal every single day.

Part of being courageously confident is giving yourself a reality check every once in a while. Your vehicle needs the fluids checked, to be fueled up, and washed periodically, and your body and goals deserve the same treatment. We need constant reflection, feedback, and awareness. Sometimes we need to reset to make sure we're aligned with our goals in the pursuit of what is setting our soul on fire. If it's not in alignment, then the answer is a heck no! If the answer is yes, then let's go!

Put your seatbelt on - it's a wild ride! Time to take some action, sister. Another mantra I got from a wise business coach: the universe likes speed. We must start taking significant action now. In order to show up courageously confident, you must invest in yourself. You must take a look in the mirror and ask yourself:

What do you desire?
  Where are you right now?
  Where do you want to be?

You know you're hungry for a better life. Are you ready to climb the mountain? You're ready for that next step, otherwise, you would not be dreaming it. Recognize the gap between where you are and where you're about to go. However, this is where fear creeps in. This is also where the OPO's creep in. Yes, that's right, OPO's - Other People's Opinions. They are screaming loudly in your head and beating you up each and every day. Your saboteur or inner critic lives inside of you and it loves to keep you isolated. It loves for you to be comfy-cozy, sitting on the couch, and hitting the snooze button. It loves for you to give up on or delay your dreams and goals.

I was recently given a powerful reminder: the average human lives to age seventy five. We only get seventy five springs, seventy five summers, seventy five falls, and seventy five winters. When you break it down, seventy five doesn't seem like a lot. I'm almost forty years old and I'm just learning this lesson? How old are you right now and when did you start to see time as sand falling through the hourglass?

You know that life is precious and no one is going to do the work for you so it's time to ignite your fire. Ask yourself the powerful questions. It's time to embrace the challenge knowing that there's going to be obstacles. We have to visualize the life we want, so we're not just reacting to what happens as we float through it. No more zombie living or frantic anxiety-driven life. There's a better way and you're made for more. You are in the driver's seat. You get to steer, so put the pedal to the metal. There's no time for a delay. We must follow our gut, our intuition and visualize the life we truly desire. We must get honest with ourselves once and for all. We must not compare ourselves to others and we must stay true to the gifts we have.

Step into your unique power. Walk into rooms more confident, more aligned, healthier, and happier. Courageous confidence is a feeling of total alignment. You know what you're put on this earth to do. You know that you're here for more. You know that you're determined and disciplined enough to go after it. You value relationships and recognize that life is precious. This body, this mind and this heart are the only ones you've got. If you want to create a legacy, you must get to work.

It's time to enjoy the journey and know who we are - deep to the core. Stay in alignment. Follow the road map, one step at a time. No matter what. Like your life depends on it, because it does.

* * *

Crews Beyond Limits Journal Prompts:

1. What is a specific challenge or obstacle that you've been avoiding or hesitant to tackle? How can you shift your perspective to see this challenge as an opportunity for growth and transformation? Reflect on the mindset shift needed to ignite your inner fire and face this challenge head-on, knowing that obstacles are stepping stones on your journey.
2. Envision your ideal life in vivid detail—what does it look like, feel like, and sound like? How can you move beyond reactive living and start proactively creating this life? Reflect on how courageous confidence aligns with this vision. What are the concrete steps you can take to walk into rooms with unwavering confidence, recognizing your purpose and determination?
3. Reflect on your unique gifts and strengths. How have you sometimes fallen into the trap of comparing yourself to others? How can you shift your focus to staying true to your own gifts and values? Consider the legacy you want to leave behind. How can you start taking action now to build that legacy and make a meaningful impact?

10

Consistency in Chaos

As the leaves began to fall and a chill filled the air in 2019, I had surgery to remove the cancer from my body. In the six months after the surgery, as I recovered, I was not able to workout, and it wreaked havoc on my nervous system. My body and brain knew this feeling all too well. I was feeling stress, overwhelm, anxiety, depression, and fear - emotions that hit me like a ton of bricks. I felt like a caged pit bull, itching to get out. This level of emotion leaves a lasting mark on our mind and in our nervous system, where it lives forever. The body will retain the stress in your brain.

It's natural for the body to respond to emotions washing over you like waves. The body will feel it first, and it may feel like you're about to burst and bite someone's head off. The goal is to manage your emotions in a positive and healthy way. It is especially important when you feel your emotions are high and your patience is low.

Even though I know this, I'm human, and I don't know about you, but I like to eat my feelings. When I'm stressed, give me comfort food: sweets and wine! I feel like I can't move and I can't go anywhere. In 2019, I spent a lot of time feeling like the caged pitbull; isolated, frustrated and angry. My healthy habits had slipped and I was uncomfortable in my skin. The only things I grabbed from my closet were baggy clothes, and most days it was something black. I did not like the person I had become. I did not recognize the person in the mirror anymore. I cried almost daily and did not want to be around anyone. I fell into a lonely spiral and felt like pizza, wine, and my husband were my only friends. These things were the only constant in my life other than calling my parents every day. I knew I needed to implement some more courageous confidence going into the new year.

As the clock struck midnight on January 1st, 2020, I realized I needed a better plan. I was bound and determined to start this year better than the last. For most of 2019, there were no good memories, no fun, no goals, because I was in survival mode. Every day I looked at my scars on my arm and leg, a constant reminder that I could not move my body the way I wanted to so desperately. I felt helpless.

I needed to take control of my mental health and keep going towards the next level version of me. I signed up for a vision board workshop online, started to sort out my thoughts, and put my dreams and goals on paper. I set a plan for all that I wanted for my life. I put it on a whiteboard magnet on the refrigerator. I looked at it every day, but I still felt stuck. l had no clue where I was going to start.

Then I got a phone call on March 17, 2020 from my coworker Rhonda who said, "Hey, you always teach these workouts and you get people to work out and run everywhere you go. All of the gyms in the country just shut down due to COVID-19. Do you think you can teach something online?" Rhonda wasn't aware of what I had been through because I had shut myself off from the outside world. I wasn't even cleared by my doctor to work out yet. I felt like my life was over, but this phone call would change my life forever.

I wanted to help people in the struggle to establish a sense of normalcy, and one way I could do that was by giving them an outlet for their mental and physical health. People had been shutting down both mentally and physically, as isolation restrictions were imposed all over the world. They could not leave their homes and relationships were strained in ways we could never have imagined before the pandemic. I asked myself a powerful question: What can I do right now with what I have? The answers came flooding into my brain.

    I was certified as a coach using a free video conferencing website. I barely knew how to use Facebook, but I decided to figure it out. I took a class to learn how to create a landing page in MailChimp, and created a Facebook event for my first virtual workout. I still have the first graphic I made in Canva. For the level of knowledge I had, I thought my marketing was perfect. My first event was "financially-free, germ-free, kids welcome. Just show up for a 30 minute workout - no equipment needed." People loved it and I had so much fun. I taught a workout at 6am and 6pm every single day during COVID from March 17th until May 30th for men, women, and children. I led dance camps, cheer camps, and running camps. I was a babysitter, friend, fitness coach, a cheerleader, and accountability partner. I built a community of people wanting to live happier and healthier during a global pandemic.

    I knew that if I was going to help anyone, I needed to show up consistently. I had the tools to help others do the same, and this gave me the motivation I needed. I helped people plan out their week. I gave classes on meal prep, time blocking, decluttering, and most importantly, my 30 minute high intensity interval training (HIIT) and kickboxing workouts. I knew we needed to help increase the intensity and the efficiency of exercise and work. This was something I learned in the military. I knew that starting my day with a workout, good nutrition, good hydration, good sleep, and recovery was the combination that provided me with a consistent foundation. It allowed me to begin working toward my goals and gave me a sense of purpose again that made me feel alive.

    I found that online teaching and coaching was more efficient than doing so in person. I began offering private goal-setting calls and vision board workshops like the one that had helped me so much a few months before. I wanted to give people hope, direction, and manageable steps to follow. I wanted to help them go after their dreams and goals for their fitness, relationships, careers, and their life. On each of these calls, we co-created a system of non-negotiables. We would map out what a typical day looked like for them. I designed a 30 day habit tracker to help develop consistency. The "next level" version of you will start to recognize what food or activity was more powerful than you. We need to ask the tough questions, such as:

What kind of life do you really want?
Are you committed to being happier and healthier?
Are you interested in leveling up?
Are you fully committed to making a change? `

Developing consistent habits is tough. Showing up every day is hard, especially during a pandemic, or when you're tired, you work from home, or you're an entrepreneur. Boundaries are blurred, and the normal 'work day' never ends. There's no set work schedule and no one to hold you accountable. How do you stay consistent? It's easier to be a permanent fixture in your living room, cozy on the couch. This was most of us at the start of the pandemic. It was fun for a few months. We watched YouTube videos, created SnapChat videos, ordered pizza more times than I'd like to admit, and watched all the shows on our streaming services. However, after a while, the fun faded, and many of us realized that we had been sedentary for too long. This is where the Crews Beyond Limits thirty-four minute mindset was born. We made a pact to put ourselves and our health first for thirty-four minutes every single day in order to reduce the stress and overwhelm of life and to live a more fulfilling one.

Part of being courageously confident is to determine and stick to our non-negotiables. Mine include movement, nutrition and hydration. We all have the same 1,440 minutes every day. I did the math. Thirty-four minutes is just two percent of your day. It takes a commitment to show up every single day, no matter what. We need to communicate this pact with ourselves with others in our life if we want to be successful. Having support and accountability is crucial. We all know we should establish a healthy routine for our body, mind, spirit, and soul. You know that your body needs food and fuel to work at optimum performance. This allows us to pour into everyone and everything else. The challenge is to develop a 'you first' mentality - you have to put on your own oxygen mask first.

    Having a vision board, or a plan, and saying you're going to be consistent and show up is great, but it's tougher to actually follow through. The truth is, we all need some accountability. We have to figure out how we are going to make our plan long term and sustainable. Fad diets, supposed quick fixes, and marketing gimmicks full of empty promises may claim you will lose weight, get stronger or healthier quickly. My high school yearbook quote said, "There is no elevator to success. You must take the stairs, one step at a time." After years of studying psychology and emotional intelligence, I now know that the brain keeps track of the times that you show up for yourself. Each time you do this, consistent momentum builds on itself. It fosters your feeling of accomplishment. It's like a bell that dings in your head every time you show up and do what you said you were going to do. That's why I love tracking my habits. You can download my free habit tracker at www.krystalorecrews.com/habittracker. Motivation is not just going to manifest. Your body and your nervous system wants to keep you safe and comfortable, and that nasty inner critic wants you to hit the snooze button and sabotage your dreams and goals. That critic will most likely tell you the seventy things that are wrong with you, including how unworthy, how out of shape, how uncoordinated, and how incapable you are. These voices will convince you that there's no way you can trust yourself to stay consistent for that long.

    Whether you show up for yourself or you cancel your workout, either way, it's not going to be comfortable. I've never regretted a workout that I showed up for. I sure as heck regretted every single workout that I canceled. My non-negotiables start in the kitchen, with my daily morning and evening routine. It is a combination of things that compound to achieve the results we desire.

The thirty-four minute mindset starts with two minutes in the morning for journaling and gratitude, goal setting, and priorities. This is mapped out in my first book, *Your Krystal Clear Life Planner, A Woman's 90 day Action Plan to Embrace Chaos and Live a Fulfilling Life!*. Next, we take action on a minimum of thirty minutes of movement per day. Lastly, each night we take two minutes to celebrate the small wins, big wins, and everything in between. It's also important to recognize the emotions that come up during the day and what got in the way of achieving our goals. Did you hit your water goal? Did you do the workout you said you were going to do? What can you do differently tomorrow? Be sure to create a system and you will begin to create a consistent pattern of courageous confident action like your life depends on it, because it does.

* * *

Crews Beyond Limits Journal & Reflection Prompts:

1. Describe your morning routine: What's the first thing you do upon waking up? How does this routine set the tone for your day ahead? Explore how self-care intertwines with your mornings—what's your skincare routine, and how does it make you feel?
2. As you consider your nutrition, share what you typically have for breakfast and how it fuels your energy. Reflect on how these practices contribute to your well-being and set the stage for a balanced and fulfilling day.

3. Dive into the factors that occasionally cause stress in your life. What are these stressors, and how do they affect your overall mindset? Shift your focus to organization—what aspects of your life do you feel need more structure? How can better organization alleviate stress and enhance your daily life? Lastly, explore the lighter side: What activities do you do for fun? How do you carve out time to enjoy these moments of leisure? Consider how these recreational pursuits contribute to your overall happiness and sense of fulfillment.

11

Run With the Pack

After I complete my morning routine and workout, my work day starts in the "command center" with two laptops, five computer screens, two ring lights, two keyboards, two mice, two sets of blue light glasses, the fancy Blue Snowball microphone, an iPhone, iPad, and my favorite digital notebook. My other favorite items include a stack of 3x5 index cards, a Sharpie, my copy of *Your Krystal Clear Life Planner* and my #CrewsBeyondLimits Habit Tracker. Lastly, my trusted sidekicks are my bottle of water, my running watch, and my AirPods. I have everything I need to stay connected, including high speed internet access with the capability to reach the world. When I get on Zoom calls and phone interviews, I'm always greeted with comments such as, "wow you have so much energy, you are so motivated and driven. How do you do it?"

The truth is that building an online business for the last six years has been an emotional roller coaster. Even with all of the connections I'm capable of making, it has been a lonely journey. I've built the recipe of my business starting with my education and experience, sprinkled with my drive and passion, and topped with my purpose and a mission to serve.

Did I choose entrepreneurship or did it choose me? I'm still not sure. Needless to say, every time I hop on a call to connect and help another human, my heart is full. Moving four times in six years is not easy. Being away from family is not easy. Making friends as adults is not easy. As an extrovert and former NFL cheerleader, I thrive around people. I love to ignite their fire and bring energy to the room. I love to empower others and put a smile on their face. In fact, my planner has a daily prompt of "who can I make smile today?"

If you're reading this message and I put a smile on your face by reading this book, please send me a message on Facebook or Instagram. Tell me what made you smile. As humans, none of us are meant to do life alone. Pay attention to extroverted entrepreneurs, trying to build an empire from a spare bedroom with no outside contact.

Early on in my entrepreneur days, I felt like a puppy, anxiously waiting for my husband to come home. I waited at the door, waited to connect, and waited to share stories about our day. Most days, when he comes home we're both mentally and physically exhausted. He gets it and he gets me. He knows that one of my core values is connection and community.

Some circumstances can leave us feeling extra lonely, unsupported, and we're left trapped inside four walls. If you're finding yourself cocooning or feeling alone in this season of your life, it might be helpful to use the Crews Beyond Limits Journal & Reflection Prompts at the end of each chapter. If we're in solitude long enough, a few things different things could happen:

1. You will cocoon, isolate yourself, and gain so much independence that you don't want to ask for help.
2. You may be so annoyed with people that you don't think anyone is there to help you.
3. You will cancel plans and stay home to work more. You might think,

"It will be worth it someday," "There's just too much work to do. Maybe I'll rest this weekend."
4. You hesitate to share your big lofty goals.
5. A few of you will build a massive empire that no one knows about.
6. Others will question what you are doing. They will not understand as they don't see all the effort behind the scenes.

My journal reflected these things each night, but I kept my head down and I kept taking steps forward with courageous confidence, knowing what's possible. The word impossible can also be read as "I'm possible." For too long, I waited for validation from friends, family, coworkers, bosses, and even strangers on the internet. This never really changed, until January of 2022, when I found my home away from home, the Lifepoint Church. I started building my relationship with God, and it has been the best decision of my life. I realized that He is the only one I need validation from. It's just Him and me, no matter what.

Maybe you're going through hard things. Maybe someone gifted this book to you, or told you it's what you need right now. Maybe you're going after your big dreams and goals. Maybe you are trying to build a business, or you're the first in your family to do something like this. Maybe you feel like the lone wolf, charging down the sidewalk, carrying a flag. It's lonely, it's dark, but it's also worth it, because it's your dream.

There are likely a million reasons to quit. The O.P.O.'s, or Other People's Opinions, try to knock us down and wear us out. Belief in yourself and taking action with courageous confidence despite the OPOs is the foundation of Crews Beyond Limits. In order to keep propelling yourself forward, it's important to not worry about limits other people are trying to place on the aspirations you have for your life. More importantly, when we are so hard on ourselves and we place limits on ourselves, we are not living out our true gifts. I feel that if you do this, you are not obeying your purpose, passion, and direction as a child of God.

You are not in complete alignment and ultimate trust. When I learned this, I realized I needed a community - a community that understands, loves, and supports me. A community that lifts me up and will cheer me on. When you find a community of like-minded people, you will thrive. This community will not tell you to scale back. They will not tell you to choose one thing or the other. They will ask, "How can I support you?" and "What can I do to help you get the message out?" This is the ultimate level of support. This is family, one that is aligned with your values: your mission, purpose, and vision. Run with this pack, and I promise you your life will improve.

We do hard things around here in the Crews Beyond Limits community.e are courageously confident, and we have fun. Results are fun, and we don't have to take ourselves so seriously. We get to come just as we are. The love and support meet you wherever you're at in your journey, wherever you are in the world, no matter what. I have built a community where everyone feels welcome, we work as a team, we empower more leaders, we have fun, and we hold each other accountable. It's important that we see things in other people that sometimes they don't even see in themselves, and we are angels to others. With our support and leadership, they will thrive. We get to show them what's possible, as we step into that next level version of ourselves; happier and healthier.

When you decide to step into the role model and leader mindset is when you share your gifts with the world. The impact will have a ripple effect, just as a stone skipping over a pond. It hits multiple times, and it could go on for miles and miles, years and years. It could change generations and influence lives globally. Sometimes change begins with one action, one step. The momentum that happens in a community provides accountability and allows others to connect on a personal level. People need to see evidence of others showing up and doing hard things amidst life struggles, challenges, heartache, grief and pain. Despite the setbacks life can throw at you, you still have a choice in how you respond. You can decide to show up anyway. You can decide to get in community with your people. This simple formula builds the momentum:

Momentum + evidence of other people doing hard things + connection = courageous confidence

This equation continues to amplify the momentum, which breeds more results. It's a combination of things that makes the system work. Life is a journey and is full of ups and downs. There are always lessons to learn. By getting in community, we gain perspective and knowledge that the storm will pass. We gain powerful insight and support while we honor the struggle. We know that with courageous confidence, we can move forward with what we've got. We know we have support. We know that our community will be there to pick us up when we need it and lift us up when we're ready.

We're not meant to do life alone. It's no fun that way! Keep showing up just as you are, wherever you're at in the world. There is a place for you. Just reach out like your life depends on it, because it does.

* * *

Crews Beyond Limits Journal Prompts:

1. Who makes up your tribe or pack, those who ignite your journey with their support? Reflect on the qualities that attract you to a community.
2. How open are you to vulnerability, sharing your challenges, and seeking help within your current network? How can this willingness contribute to your growth?
3. Consider your impact on your community. How can you amplify this effect to empower others? Reflect on your current connections—what shifts can you make to enhance your life, business, or relationships? How will these changes contribute to your growth and the growth of those around you?

12

The Finish Line

As your courageous confidence builds, you will start to feel unstoppable, unshakable, and unbreakable. Once you implement this standard for your life and you know who you are to the core, you will see yourself more consistently showing up, and leveling up in all areas of your life. This confidence helps you stand a bit taller. It helps you feel sexier, healthier, and happier. You are going to want to be more visible. You've pushed through so many hard things, and you found a supportive community that will cheer you on and lift you up. When you ask for help, they're there. When you need to lend a hand, you're always there to be a leader.

Now, as you start seeing results, people start to notice and they feel your passion. They see your drive. They see you as more confident, more energetic, and you smile more. You shine a little bit differently. They will compliment you. You'll start to hear things like "what's different about you? or "Whatever you're doing, it's working!" or "Wow, you've got this glow to your face." That's the special love glow. You're falling in love with yourself. This discovery of self-love with courageous confidence is so incredible that you want to shout from the rooftops.

This ripple effect of your courageous confidence has an impact on your life and you're feeling it. Perhaps it's the award you won, or the ten pounds that you lost. Maybe you fit in your skinny jeans again or you're rocking that romper you thought you'd never dare wear. Maybe you're getting promoted, or you're buying the house of your dreams. Maybe you are retiring from the military after several years of dedication. Thank you for your service. No matter what amazing results you are seeing, you are a rockstar!

You're getting out of toxic relationships and finally developing healthy ones again. You're breaking down walls and barriers. Maybe you're starting a business or writing that book. You're getting on that stage, and you want to tell everyone you know! You've worked so hard. You've shown up daily, taking consistent actions, even when it was tough, when you wanted to snooze, when you didn't want to work out, when you didn't want to make those calls, when you didn't want to be in the workshops. You traveled when you didn't want to leave home and your family. You're finally feeling the impact of all the networking events and times you showed up in spaces you never felt you belonged in. You have a supportive community that cheers you on.

It was all worth it, and now it's time to celebrate. But somehow, you're still in the cage, silent, and frozen. Deep down, you know you're worth it. In practice it's so much easier to celebrate everybody else. We love to plan the parties for everyone else, to buy them gifts, to give them praise. When it comes to your own time to shine, somehow you aren't as deserving of a celebration. You open a post on Facebook or Instagram to celebrate how good you feel but you pause. You may start typing a message with a cute photo, then edit it ten times, only to erase it. You think, "Nah, they'll think I'm bragging again".

Instead, you try with little things. You reward yourself with a pedicure, by going for a walk, or going out for ice cream. Maybe you go out to dinner and drinks with a loved one, friend, or business partner and casually bring up your latest accomplishments. Those are easy. Somehow something keeps holding us back from sharing our success more widely.

What are you afraid of? Most likely, it's those pesky O.P.O.'s about you showing up and going after your dreams. They will see you being fully aligned in all of your passion and your purpose. You're an amazing human and more improved version of you. You transformed your life by showing up no matter what. Well my friend, I'm here to tell you that you're worth it. You're worth every ounce of celebration, deep to the core for as long as you want to celebrate and however you want to do it. You get to design the life that you desire. You get to have your own self care regimen. You get to work out, and you get to have the time for you. You get to have laughs, and you get to receive the compliments. You get to have accountability, support and you get to have the love. You get to set the boundaries, and you get to say no to the things that don't serve you. Also, you get to say "Heck yes!" to the things that are setting your soul on fire. You get to invest in yourself, and you see so much more for yourself.

Despite this self discovery, we still sit in fear, and sometimes will have moments where we shrink back down, back to old habits.. Maybe you feel different now, and it feels foreign. Maybe you have changed too much. Maybe you're thinking "will they like me? Will they still support me? Will they like this next version of me? What if I outgrow them? I won't have any friends and I'll be alone again." This endless cycle wreaks havoc on our nervous system, like a hurricane plowing through a Caribbean island. It may feel like a vicious cycle. Fear holds us back, it keeps us stuck, and fear keeps us playing small. I want to kick that nasty inner critic out and punch her squarely in the face. This is where the courage to take action must kick in despite the fear. When things are uncomfortable and we have fear, we can either panic, shut down, retreat, or fuel forward with massive action. This massive action is called courageous confidence. It's knowing yourself, trust, drive, a movement. We practice these tools daily thanks to the Crews Beyond

Limits Virtual HIIT camp program, which teaches kickboxing and karate moves for self defense cardio kicking, intense workout to shred, tone, and shape your body. It's cheaper than anger management, and it's great for preventative medicine and care for your body. In our community, we work on kicking our inner critic to the curb daily. When we move our body, we feel more courageous, confident, and capable of anything!

When you implement the courageous confidence model, you can go after your dreams and goals and show up for the party. Even if it's a dance party in your closet, dance like no one's watching. When you show up in true alignment with your values and goals and put your dreams, passion, and purpose all together, this is true freedom. You get to shout from the rooftops and share your unique gifts with the world. Yes, you too.

When I started my business in 2017, I felt as though no one understood what I was doing. I don't fault them for it, because working remote and starting an online business before COVID really wasn't a popular thing. Had I listened to the O.P.O.'s, I would not be writing this book. For those naysayers out there who think I'm bragging, allow me to introduce you to the Crews Beyond Limits version and definition of bragging: "celebrating yourself while putting someone else down in the same sentence." If you're not doing that, then you're not bragging. Keep shining sister, and chances are the haters will not spend any time on you, because they're only thinking about themselves...and they sure as heck won't read this book all the way to the end.

So, my friend, if you're still with me, thank you. You're my kind of person. I'm in your corner as your personal and professional cheerleader. I'm here to tell you, you are worthy of celebration daily. We celebrate ourselves in the Krystal Clear Life Planner every single day. In my entries, in the Krystal Clear Life Planner, I celebrate the big wins, the small wins, and everything in between. I celebrate the water I drink, the workouts I accomplish, and how I showed up for other people. I practice affirmations. I practice affirmations which tell my body and brain that I am worthy, I am made for more, and I am a role model. Even as your life tour guide, I'm navigating the roadmap of life along with you. along with you. I hope that after reading this, you have established more courageous confidence to take massive action in your fitness, career, business, relationships, and your life. I want to be a personal and professional source for you, your results, and your life. I want you to feel like a million bucks.

When I was younger, I was at the beach and I was told that my nickname was MDB, because I looked like a Million Dollar Babe. I felt I had all the confidence in the world, but I wasn't able to receive that compliment. It wasn't until I was in true alignment with my values and freedom that I realized what feeling like that meant. Being a million dollar babe is about having a foundation of courageous confidence. This cultivated true alignment of my passion, power, momentum, self care, boundaries, accountability and celebration.

I began to see massive transformation from the power of stepping up, paving the way, and creating a community that I so desperately needed. So did the rest of the world. Last year I leveled up even more, and added in person events to Crews Beyond Limits. I designed the ultimate six day all inclusive wellness retreat in a villa on the top of the mountain in Costa Rica. I knew that my community needed to meet in person. They needed to invest in themselves. They needed me to pour into them like the Queens that they are, as they don't plan to take care of anything. They're loved, welcomed, supported and celebrated. This experience led these women through a transformation, a beautiful sisterhood, and memories to last a lifetime.

Through adventure, self care, self love, self exploration, and exercise we must celebrate life, especially as we continue to pour into other humans, giving them the tools for self love, self care, and clarity to revive themselves, so they can thrive in life. This is the ripple effect of leadership. My clients show up willing and ready for self discovery, empowerment, and community. They know they are here for more, that I'm in their corner, and they're never alone.

All you have to do is show up no matter what, like your life depends on it, because it does. Keep celebrating sister. You're worth it.

***

Crews Beyond Limits Journal Prompts:

1. Reflect on your journey and goals. Imagine the transformative impact of having a coach or mentor by your side, guiding you forward. What would it mean to you to have personalized support and expertise? Embrace the power of seeking help and envision how partnering with a coach or mentor could propel you towards your aspirations. Consider the first step you can take today to explore this opportunity and open the door to transformative growth.
2. How can you tap into your courageous confidence to ignite your goals? Reflect on a specific goal you've been hesitant to pursue. How would approaching it with unwavering self-assuredness change your approach and propel you forward?
3. Envision your version of success. How can your courageous confidence be the driving force that leads you there? Reflect on instances where you've felt this confidence, and how it impacted your outcomes. What steps can you take today to align your mindset with the success you aspire to achieve?

13

The Resilience Revolution

As we wrap up our exploration of "The Road to Resilience: 5 Ways to Have Courageous Confidence in Seasons of Change," let's pause to reflect on the profound path we've navigated together. Throughout this book, we've ventured into the depths of the messy middle—the juncture where challenges, growth, and strength collide. We dove into the importance of embracing vulnerability, pursuing dreams with unwavering confidence, and cultivating a resilient spirit that propels us forward.

As we conclude, I want to highlight that your journey to resilience is an ongoing odyssey. Life's ever-shifting seasons require a constant commitment to personal growth and empowerment. While I've shared my experiences, lessons, and the Courageous Confidence Model, this is merely the compass and to your own adventure. My hope is that you paved new pathways and possibilities for your next chapter of your life.

The essence of resilience lies within your grasp. It's all about the persistent belief in your potential, the dedication to consistency, the power of community, and the celebration of your accomplishments—no matter how small. Remember that the messy middle is where growth flourishes, wisdom is extracted, and untapped strength resides.

As you forge ahead, keep your core values at the forefront of your journey. Cultivate confidence by setting ambitious goals and taking actionable steps toward them. Infuse consistency into your daily routines, nurturing your physical and mental well-being. Build meaningful connections that provide support and accountability along your path. And above all, take joy in each stride you take toward your dreams.

For ongoing empowerment, explore https://www.krystalorecrews.com a treasure trove of resources to aid your growth and resilience journey. Stay connected with me and the Crews Beyond Limits community as we navigate life's twists and turns together.

In line with our journey, I encourage you to embrace the Courageous Confident Action Plan:

1. Identify Your Core Values: Ground yourself in what truly matters.
2. Set Goals and Vision: Utilize tools like vision board workshops or planners to get Krystal Clear on your aspirations.
3. Stay Consistent and Disciplined: Establish unshakable standards, tracking your progress utilizing tools such as the Crews Beyond Limits Planner and Habit Trackers.
4. Join a Supportive Community: Surround yourself with like-minded individuals for mutual support and encouragement.
5. Celebrate Your Success: Document your progress and revel in the triumphs within your planner.

Additionally, explore the range of offerings within Crews Beyond Limits:

- Join us at the next Crews Beyond Limits Vision Board Workshop: https://www.krystalorecrews.com/visionboard
- Utilize the Habit Tracker to monitor your progress: https://www.krystalorecrews.com/habittracker
- Engage with the free community for camaraderie and guidance:

https://www.facebook.com/groups/crewsbeyondlimits
- Immerse yourself in the transformative Bombshell Confidence Bootcamp Course: https://www.krystalorecrews.com/bombshellbootcamp
- Sweat and Connect with the Crews Beyond Limits Virtual HIITcamp Fitness Community for inspiration and motivation: https://www.krystalorecrews.com/crewsbeyondlimitsgroupfitness
- Join the ultimate holistic health experience, The Million Dollar Body Academy Course: https://www.krystalorecrews.com/milliondollarbodyacademy
- Immerse yourself in a self-care transformation experience with the Crews Beyond Limits Retreats(private & corporate tours available): https://www.krystalorecrews.com/revivalretreat
- Do you want to book me to speak or give a wellness or leadership workshop for your team? Contact me https://www.krystalorecrews.com/speaker

As you continue your journey, remember that you're not only crafting your story but also becoming a testament to resilience, empowerment, and authenticity. The messy middle is where transformation flourishes, vulnerability turns into strength, and resilience becomes second nature.

With heartfelt gratitude and enthusiasm for your ongoing growth, I'm always in your corner, Cheers!

Krystalore Crews Author, Speaker, Resilience Advocate

Rating and Review: If this book resonated with you, I'd be honored if you took a moment to rate and review it. Your feedback will help others discover the transformative power of resilience. Additionally, I'm excited to share that 10% of the proceeds from this book supports scholarships for female Veterans and Military Spouses. These scholarships aim to empower them on their journey to greatness during their own seasons of change. Finally, consider gifting this book to someone who may benefit from its message—a gesture that could spark their own journey to empowerment. Thank you for being an integral part of the Crews Beyond Limits movement!

About the Author

Krystalore Crews, the driving force behind Crews Beyond Limits, is an unstoppable entrepreneur, motivational speaker, and resilience expert. Originally from Buffalo, NY, and now based in Louisville, KY, Krystalore's life has been defined by movement and transformation. As both a military service member and a dedicated wife, she embodies courage, resilience, and tenacity.

A true high performer, Krystalore is on a mission to empower individuals worldwide to devote just 34 minutes per day to their wellbeing. Specializing in HIIT and kickboxing, she shares her message of empowerment with women, inspiring them to prioritize themselves and their health.

Krystalore's passion for personal development is palpable. Her talks, workshops, and coaching sessions are not only informative but also engaging and energizing. She champions values such as community, integrity, and hard work, which resonate deeply within her Crews Beyond

Limits movement.

Drawing from her wealth of experience in conquering life's challenges, Krystalore authored "The Road to Resilience: 5 Ways to Have Courageous Confidence in Seasons of Change." This groundbreaking book unveils her Courageous Confidence Model—a transformative blueprint that empowers readers to pursue their dreams unapologetically, even amidst uncertainty.

Additionally, Krystalore is the author of "Your Krystal Clear Life Planner: A Woman's 90 Day Action Plan to Embrace Chaos and Live a Fulfilling Life!" This comprehensive guide offers practical strategies for women to embrace chaos, achieve their goals, and live a life filled with purpose.

Connect with Krystalore on her website at www.krystalorecrews.com, where you can access resources, workshops, and stay updated on her latest ventures. Join the Crews Beyond Limits movement and embark on a journey of resilience and empowerment.

For speaking engagements, media inquiries, or coaching sessions, reach out to Krystalore Crews at krystalore@thecrewscoach.com or visit www.krystalorecrews.com.

Follow Krystalore:

You can connect with me on:
- http://www.krystalorecrews.com
- https://www.facebook.com/krystalore
- https://www.instagram.com/thecrewscoach
- https://www.linkedin.com/in/krystalore-crews
- https://www.youtube.com/@krystalore
- https://www.pinterest.com/krystalorecrews

www.ingramcontent.com/pod-product-compliance
Lightning Source LLC
Chambersburg PA
CBHW021117080526
44587CB00010B/550